Dearly
Beloved

30 days in the OSHO ashram,

discovering the soul of a spiritual enterprise.

Published by White Tea Studios.

www.whiteteastudios.com | info@whiteteastudios.com

Classification: (1) Travel. (2) Spirituality. (3) Business and Marketing.

This book is designed to provide context and accurate information regarding the subject matter. It is sold with the understanding that the author or publisher is not engaged in rendering spiritual, travel or other professional advice. If such advice or assistance is required, the services of a competent professional should be sought out.

- Adapted from the *Declaration of Principles* adopted by the Committee of Publishers and Associations, and the Committee of the America Bar Association.

As far as the author and publisher are aware, designations, titles and references to books, videos, discourses or talks that are referenced in this book are stated as such and remain the property of the copyright or trademark claimant.

Credits

Cover and interior design: Yousuf Tilly. Additional graphic elements: freepik.com & Sergey Kandakov. Fonts: PixelBuddha.net.

This book is available at a discount for bulk purchases in electronic, print or audio formats.

For further information, email: info@whiteteastudios.com

For my parents,

who taught me

how to give.

Preface

Consult a mystic.

For what you're about to read, I did my best to paint a useful picture, but I'm not currently levitating, walking on water, or downloading wisdom from the cosmos. I'm just a regular Joe who enjoys a smile on my face. Mystics can teach you the art of putting one on yours.

Consult them.

To the seekers, I hope you find what you're looking for. To the found, I hope you'll continue to guide.

REFERENCES

See a list of teachers and centres that you can travel to at the end of this book.

Also included in the reference section are resource links that you may find beneficial.

ACKNOWLEDGEMENTS

Thanks to those in my reading group, who assisted with the editing of this book. You know who you are, as do you WAMmers who graciously shared your time with me. We had some good laughs, didn't we!

Enjoy the read!

@yousuftilly

#DearlyBeloved

Dearly Beloved

By Yousuf Tilly

Chapter One

Dearly beloved, what follows here is somewhat akin to finding out the truth about the Easter Bunny. Yes, fantasies don't exist sadly, but realities do. Billions of them in fact, each hidden in plain view behind the eyeballs of other people, animals and insects. Like your own life, each of theirs is a world unto its own too, and it's only natural to wonder what on Earth we're all doing here. Thus was born the search for meaning, in man at least, for I've yet to come across dogs or cats who've authored books on the subject. No, the animal kingdom doesn't need any motivational books because those creatures simply live, and don't we all just love them for the little joys that they inspire?

Caveman once awoke to find a ball of fire rising in the sky. Instead of fearing the Armageddon, he rejoiced. The daylight was an opportunity to settle the rumble in his tummy and, as soon as he did, the sun set. The echoes of a million creatures hiding in the darkness of night suddenly accosted caveman. Instead of reaching for his club though, caveman became enchanted by the warm glow radiating from the white ball in the sky, and those were the very beginnings of dance. He closed his eyes and swayed along with the ocean in which all of existence was floating. Caveman wasn't confused about his purpose in life, or who to gratify. Before God, morality and the incessant stream of opinions on social media, natural man too enjoyed the liberty of taking life as it comes.

"It is everyone's birth-right," I heard a sage once say.

Simple freedoms like those sound just like the exotic holiday we all need from contemporary life and, I suppose for that very reason, it should also be asked if that is what we want to hear?

I began wondering about that while answering emails about a week into the *Work as Meditation* programme. WAM it was called for short, and saying it out loud was pretty much the experience of finding every email in my inbox begun with the salutation 'Dearly Beloved'. Images of utopia flashed in my mind, though I come from a world in which slogans like 'live-laugh-love' have been turned into hashtags and bandied about like designer handbags. The meaning of things is not always clear nowadays, and that left me staring at the emails, betwixt by whether the salutations were written with a genuine sentiment or were just the social convention of the commune I was working in.

And India is a place that can be survived only if you set aside all the assumptions you have about life.

Travelling there wasn't even on my bucket-list, yet there I was, **surrounded by a** billion strangers. I **arrived one sweltering** afternoon outside Lohegaon Airport after a journey that lasted 24 hours. All I needed was a ride to complete it, which became a problem when my taxi driver didn't like the look of my MasterCard. I got out of the car, cursing for not having changed some currency back in Delhi. An airport official pointed me in the direction of an ATM, which happened to be offline, and led me right back to him. Literally ten paces beyond the doorway where he stood was a Bureau de Change. The official shook his head the way Indians do. Without a valid travel ticket, I wasn't allowed back into the airport, he explained in broken English. I ignored him while whistling in broken Hindi to the clerk at the Bureau de Change, but she quickly turned away when the official grunted and pushed me aside with his rifle.

There and then I decided that India wasn't a place to be loved or hated. It needed to be navigated. And so, with the giant airport clock ticking away, I made a seat of my backpack to let the official know that I could go nowhere else. We were stuck with each other.

A man with a thick moustache soon arrived. The airport official saluted him then, after exchanging a few words, kicked my bag as if he too thought it a nuisance. The official and I both waited for the moustache to turn the corner before staring at each other. I assumed this was the end of my protest but, to my surprise, got a grunt to say that the coast was clear. Moments later, I was standing at the Bureau de Change, having Rupees doled out into my hands. After the clerk tallied up the stack, she held on to the last note and waved it with a smile that suggested the official deserved a tip.

Ah! …until then I had assumed that he was just being kind.

In the taxi to Koregaon Park, I tossed out all the travel literature I had on India. When I asked the driver where the Agha Khan Mosque was, he replied "five minutes", which didn't sound like a suburb of Pune to me. Trying again, I asked where MG Road was and he replied "very long". It struck me then that, with a billion people clogging up the roads in the world's biggest democracy, it was more useful to quantify distance in time. Labels like *kilometres*, which are usually used to make sense of our world, didn't really apply there. In India, a natural organisation has taken over. Some might call it chaos, but my driver thought of it as the country's greatest gift.

I discovered what he meant when pointing to the opposite side of the dual-carriageway we were travelling on. He turned our little rickshaw sharply into the oncoming traffic, never mind the truck that was speeding toward us, and rolled casually across the road to the spot I had indicated. I pinched myself to ensure that I was indeed still alive, and there it was, the fresh perspectives on life that so many travel to India for. My driver threw his head over his shoulder, laughing through his tobacco-stained teeth, and told me that self-discovery was "baksheesh". He then stuck his hand out and said that everything else in India would cost me a few Rupees.

I dragged my rucksack back upon my shoulders and hopped out of the rickshaw on Lane 1, Koregaon Park. There I stood a moment to behold the great black edifice…Thunder!

My quest had led me there without any clue as to what to expect, so I figured the obvious next step was to follow the ramp up to the ominous sign that read 'Welcome Centre'. Little did I know that I was, like an unwitting Bilbo Baggins, stepping through a portal into a whole new world.

The next morning started early. Strolling along a stone pathway upon which it snowed tiny green leaves, the ancient tree-tops filtered-out the daylight into a hodgepodge of sunbeams dancing upon the ground. I imagined myself in one of those monasteries up in the mountains, thousands of years ago. Raju, the resident cat, watched me meditatively as I made the journey to the main campus. Along the way, I spied into the windows of Krishna House where classic Barcelona chairs, Apple Mac's and colourful abstract artworks painted by the founder himself broke the stark white interior. The mosaic path ended in a plaza with a waterfall serving as the backdrop to a glass pyramid. I stopped there to take it all in. The entire campus was finished in shiny black marble tiles that ran along straight lines into a clean post-modernism vibe. It looked like a Stanley Kubrick sci-fi movie, complete with every denizen in maroon robes, but this place existed long before the future. It was the site of the original human experiment that integrated economics, community and spirituality.

Well, that's the official story.

The true rhythm of this place was flashing at me from beyond the tall bamboo trees that walled the plaza from Buddha Grove, a marble-floored stadium. There, I caught glimpses of more maroon. People were swaying with reckless abandon to a catchy dance tune that sounded familiar, but got caught on the tip of my tongue while I watched them twirling upon their toes, arms spread out wide. The expressions on their faces told tales of joy, sorrow and every human experience in between. It was enchanting to see them so lost on an ordinary morning, like one of those quotes about 'dancing like no one was watching' had suddenly come alive.

It was a striking contrast to 9am in the ordinary world.

That usually consists of spending an hour commuting when you could be sleeping, only to arrive at a desk left messy from having worked till late the previous night, and finally clearing it up to start all over again. Coffee, you may think, will give you the courage to endure, but a stiff drink is really what you'll need if ever you projected that thought.

That life usually plays out as being physically at work but distracted by the milk not to be forgotten on the way home. Without focus the days get longer, which leads to dropping comatose on the couch to recover by bingeing on increasingly violent television. On a weekly basis this ritual develops into intoxicating habits that help to both forget the gruelling week and dream of a better one starting the next Monday. That pattern of life becomes fifty years of work rewarded by being incarcerated on yet another couch in an arrangement called retirement. As a long-term strategy, it's safe, but it also sounds like the early grave many people complain about. It feels like you're not living, and the need to escape becomes rather urgent.

That's why 9am in the ordinary world is all about power.

Those dancers, on the other hand, were all letting go. If I told you that their dance was a meditation to transform our warring and poverty-stricken world you may smirk, but consider a typical newscast:

PEACE! Protesters shout with their fists thrown high-up in the air.

We are a culture that expresses our anger because we all know that no man is an island, and that wars affect us all economically, socially, and sometimes even personally. Our disillusionments with the world though have a life of their own. They surreptitiously turn into, say, shouting at telemarketers, who then go home to proverbially kick the dog. Expressing our anger unwittingly contributes to the wars we detest because war is simply mass anger. The influence of cause-and-effect allows resentment to multiply across the entire fabric of life as it is true that no man is an island. To recognise that we aren't separate from the problems of the world is the first step towards change, and it relies on personal responsibility.

That was the premise on which this place was built, and it was a whole new life that was being spun out of that dance. Those dancers were manifesting the vision of a new man - one who is as wealthy as he wants to be without, but is first rich within. *Zorba the Buddha* is what they call it. It's a prototype of a natural man upon whom they intended to build a new world. He reflects man's true capabilities, and the peak of all human experience. It's not even a revolutionary notion, just a forgotten one. Through the ages, men like Pythagoras, Lao Tzu and Rumi have all spoken about a phenomenon known as 'enlightenment'.

Quite simply, it is the experience of being switched on.

I found my own foot tapping to the possibility, that is until my mind finally caught up and recognised the song being danced to was none other than 'Hotel California'. Now I'm not one for omens. For me, tarot cards are spiritual porn. But, back in the seventies, that song led to much speculation about an actual place in California connected to Anton La Vey, author of the *Satanic Bible*. Its most famous lyrics are that 'you can check out any time you like, but you can never leave!'

I immediately recalled a friend who teased that she wasn't expecting me back from India as it sounded like I was joining a cult.

Don Healy, who wrote the song, explained that it was about the excesses of capitalism, and the dark pit of meaninglessness that materialism could trap you in.

The American Dream, however, remains the USA's greatest export, as living to the standard of middle-class America is one of the most ubiquitous ambitions the world over. It is the very definition of success that many people **crave,** so you could say that most of the working-world belongs to a cult anyway. 'Hotel California' was like a warning to them, and those dancers suddenly didn't look all that meditative anymore. I zoomed-in to see if they had their middle-fingers stuck out to the world.

"Welcome to the Osho International Meditation Resort!"

That's how Kala introduced herself. She came from Guest-Care, and found me easily since I was the only person on campus not wearing a maroon robe. "Not yet!" she quipped from behind her oversized nerdy glasses. That was a loaded statement, one that prompted me to ask if she thought WAM was just trumped-up hullabaloo, or an actual valuable experience for her. She was at the end of a three-month stint in the **programme,** but instead of satisfying my curiosity, Kala just rolled her big brown eyes. She walked briskly on while I kept pace with the hard facts she was instructed to dispense.

At first, it was all practical. I learnt what to eat, where to jive, and all about the stultifying laundry process.

But then Kala painted me a picture of the place back in the seventies, when the world was first introduced to the revolutionary new meditations that simplified the teachings of Sufi's, Yogi's and wacky mystics like Gurdjieff. It seemed that people have always been searching for themselves amidst the noise in their heads, but as opposed to solving the problem by acquiring things that helped them to feel safe, the purpose of this place was to silence the noise itself.

On offer then are meditations that help you to resolve unconscious repressions by having you laughing, crying and silent for a week each respectively. Another called *Born Again* takes you back to childhood, while *Gibberish* is a meditation that spring-cleans your mind of all the crap you've gathered since. You can explore your previous lives, use art to peer into your subconscious, or simply get a massage if all that sounds too crazy.

Kala called it a 'Mystery School', a sort of real-life *Hogwarts* for muggles who wanted to understand themselves. Personal freedom was their only goal.

At the height of the ashram's popularity however, the world was shocked by a documentary that showed naked people howling at each other in a padded room. From what I understand, it's a therapy based on Arthur Janov's *Primal Scream*, which helps to consciously relive past traumas so that they can be released from your psyche and stop bothering you. According to the documentary, black eyes and broken bones ensued.

If that's what spiritual gurus are preaching, it's easy to see why so many people would rather opt for a lifetime of disciplined work instead of indulging in self discovering.

One of the recent entrants on the scene, Sadhguru Jaggi Vasudev, explained that we are so entrenched in what we believe is a sane way of life that we would rather run for the hills than experience ourselves at full potential. The things that happen at ashrams are merely activities to keep us engaged, thereby allowing some time for us to grow. I suppose it doesn't really matter what route you take to self-discovery as, if you don't know where Xanadu is, there isn't much choice other than trusting the Sherpa who knows the way.

The proof, after all, is in the pudding.

And so, I took a spoonful. At the Galleria, Bupendra took one glance at me and guessed the size of my robe. POOF! I emerged from the change-room, maroon like everyone else. That's when I mustered up the courage to ask Kala again, flat out, if WAM was just trumped up hullabaloo or actually a valuable experience for her.

Kala stopped abruptly to hit me with a Zen paradox. "This is not an ashram!" she exclaimed.

I glanced at the statue of Buddha floating over a pool of **water, but** he had nothing to say. Then again, he did spend his life preaching the benefits of silence.

Kala went on to evade my question again by explaining that this wasn't a monastic community, and there was no one leading the religious retreat. It was buffet-style **spirituality; the** personally-responsible approach. My curiosity unsatisfied, I wondered if this was yet another fact she was instructed to dispense. She smiled, I smiled, and then Kala handed me over to Carla in the WAM office.

Damn! What were the odds of everyone I was meeting at the ashram having the same name? I must be in a cult, I mused.

Carla however turned out to be a bubbly and energetic New Yorker who navigated the complicated spreadsheets in the WAM office like Christopher Columbus. After the admin was completed, we sauntered over to the hospital next door to the ashram for ten-rupee chai and cashew biscuits. While watching a kid pull flowers out of the ground, Carla answered the question that Kala dodged.

Carla came to India to enrol in WAM after being part of a small band of determined people who put their backs into a project that turned into a widely-successful dotcom. It was a moving experience to have built something so significant, but the cost of attaining the success that millions dream of made her question what the point of it all was?

"Working in New York", she said, "was like working in New York," and then she added, "y'know?" in that sing-song voice North-Americans have.

I understood perfectly. Nothing fails like success, and Ghandi put it into perspective well. He said that "everything you do is insignificant, but it's very important that you do it". That's a drastically different take on 'passion', the cornerstone of western life.

Passion is, in fact, an estimated $13-billion industry called Personal Development (PD). It thrives on helping people shake off the feeling that they're not living by offering visions of success, health and nurturing relationships. As a system, it also provides the actionable steps to achieve those visions so, in a way, PD is busy creating a new man just like the ashram aims to do. The only difference is that it's for people who have become cynical toward the traditional establishments of spirituality that have historically been dispensing that advice. All the same, it's just another method of finding meaning in life; one that hinges on discipline.

For it to work though, you need an ideal to keep you motivated. Without an ideal, throwing tractor tyres around in CrossFit seems pointless. Ideals then help to justify the monumental effort required to claim success in our competitive world but, as Carla pointed out, it's easy to get stuck on the treadmill of defending those ideals to maintain the success we fight so hard for. Soon our worlds become insular and, in that way, success can become a cage. It was a rather disappointing experience for her.

What Carla was really looking for was in the hands of that naughty child, who was now being scolded by his mum. The kid turned to us with dirty hands, snot running from his nose, and clueless as to why his bewilderment had so effortlessly put a smile on our faces. He glowed with the sense of wonder we once felt as children ourselves. It was innocence that radiated from him, and the unconditional acceptance that wafted through the garden **helped** us to feel part of something bigger.

Think of any place where you are completely accepted for who you are and you'll notice just how different **you are in that space.** There's no substitute for connection, which is quite contradictory to distinguishing yourself through success.

Very subtly, it dawned on me that this was why Kala couldn't answer my question. She could only give me the facts that helped me make of it what I would. Connecting to the essence of what went on in the ashram was entirely up to me.

About that, I already had an interesting encounter.

Earlier that day, I was sat down by Leelaq, who dropped my WAM application into her lap and assigned me to work in the Welcome Centre. This was the same Welcome Centre that Kala mentioned having begged to be transferred from. It was also the place where Carla helped out occasionally, and knew of a storm brewing there between staff and the coordinator that no one liked.

I protested, only to find that maroon robes weren't the only thing that was compulsory in the ashram. My choices as to where I worked in WAM were being made for me because everyone serviced the commune in some way or the other. My inclusion in WAM depended on me toeing the line and, to encourage me, Leelaq tossed the 'S' word at me.

It was a big word, and typical of the controversy that plagued the Osho commune.

Their history can be summed up as challenging the Indian authorities on taxation, and then escaping to

America where they transplanted the commune, only to end up being accused of the largest bio-terror attack on US soil and a conspiracy to murder amongst other mayhem. A fleet of 93 Rolls Royce's were left as collateral damage when the whole Oregon episode imploded, and they returned to **Pune claiming that their** master was poisoned by Ronald Reagan's government as the last straw in proving that their vision for a new humanity could only be enjoyed by those intelligent enough to understand it.

'Surrender', you see, was a rather big word. And to whom was the question?

The Zen master who established the ashram was Rajneesh, a man who people addressed as the Bhagwan, or God, long before his name was Osho. Rajneesh isn't even his real name. It's a moniker that translates to 'Prince of the Night' **and** was given to him by his family because he was always disruptive, even as a child. So many name changes didn't bode well for his credibility, but Rajneesh's notoriety was on the rise long before the commune's antics.

He penned the book *'From Sex to Super-Consciousness'*, which wasn't a book about sex, but sex does nevertheless sell, and Rajneesh's reputation as the 'Sex Guru' attracted a global following. Once people arrived at his feet though, they remained in India as his devotees not for Rajneesh's lewd impressions, but rather for his incredibly insightful words about life, you, and me.

You could say that Rajneesh was about the only Indian who didn't shake his head the way the other billion do, and the rebellion he instigated was no joke either.

It was about how humanity organised themselves. You simply can't expect to earn a living and still go home to bake your own bread. It's just not practical, so we are all interdependent on each other for a decent standard of living. To facilitate that, the ancient world divided themselves into four classes of society.

The priests supplied religion as the law, as governments do today, and that was supported by an economy kept in motion by the merchant class. To protect the interests of all, warriors were charged with keeping order, as policemen do today, and the last division was the slave class who serviced the needs of the entire community in exchange for their basic needs.

Western movies reflect this social stage of humanity well. If you trotted into town on your horse, you'd find a row of retail stores on one side, the saloon on the other, and a church at the end. This layout reflects the human needs for implements, relationships, and meaning respectively. All of it was overseen by the sheriff, whose offices were located right up front. Order was the raison d'etre of human society back then, naturally because going back to scavenging in the bushes was too difficult.

Rather rebelliously, Osho challenged the very core of this structure. He pointed out that religion has always been administered by ordinary men who've only claimed to be God's vice-regents on Earth but, thus far, no God has arrived to claim humanity as His creation. And so, in practice, the idea of God was not merely an instrument of control, but was also one rife with abuse.

Osho also wasn't the only one to note that a belief in a god wasn't a requirement for humanity's wellbeing. Buddha too fought the Brahmins, the priest class of his time, on the same principle. If you listen carefully to other men like Krishnamurti or Eckhart Tolle, they too are saying that quality of life is lost by outsourcing our hopes for success, peace or love, to the great guy in the sky. They too advocate personal responsibility rather than looking up to the heavens and wondering if Charlton Heston is looking back at you.

To Osho, the idea of a God was merely a projection of the human mind for its need to survive, and was why the concept of God was riddled with the very basic contradiction of being astonishingly merciful and kind on one hand, yet undeniably vengeful on the other if His system of morality was not conformed to. You can see now why there was a need for sheriffs in the ancient world.

There's a difference between believing in an idea and an actual knowing. Test it out right now by asking yourself if you are, in fact, holding this text with your hand, or just believe that you are?

That sort of provocation is what made Osho, and other enlightened men of his ilk, so compelling. They were talking about what was real as opposed to the fiction of beliefs. While I cannot say whether Osho was enlightened or not, I don't think it really matters all that much when you consider that he was a man who was unapologetically himself.

That's the personal dignity we all want for ourselves.

It was also something that hit me like a ton of bricks while in the company of friends whom I've endeared for many years. I crept up to the door to surprise them with a fancy new drink I had as a treat for them, only to find them whispering rather unflattering things about me inside. Boo! I surprised them when their conversation was over. They instantly cheered the bottle I brought along with me and, after filling everyone's glasses, I sat down alongside them with a smile. By then, I understood why they were my friends. All of us had that ugly mask stuck over our own faces, and since then, integrity has fascinated me to no end.

It was the mystery I had come to this ashram to solve since my quest had thus far proven religious morality to be an inadequate tool for the job. Religion frames life by the polarities of good and evil, heaven and hell, or closer to home, pleasure and pain. But a binary compass is ineffective to navigate a life that constitutes a myriad of greys. Even my three-year-old nephew knows that. He once quipped, rather frankly I might add, that eating his 'Zoo-Biscuits' before his chicken meant that both would still go down the hatch anyway. It was an astonishing insight into how our personal truths can't ever be borrowed, not even from the Pope.

Really, in life, who else is there to rely on besides yourself?

And that's when I began to appreciate clarity, rather than the confidence we so often are encouraged to cultivate, as the ultimate power in life. For all the babble thrown around as to the meaning of life, it's actually a very simple thing. It is asking what to do with yourself every single morning when you wake up, as no one ever knows if their eyes will open again after closing them the night before. Those little decisions turn into our lives, and how we repeatedly answer that one simple question becomes the life we create. The meaning of life is what we choose to do, and that depends entirely upon your interpretation of things. Confidence then is not the appropriate tool to navigate life with. Clarity is.

Perhaps Leelaq too couldn't see that, by having me surrender my choice, she was asking me to pretend that this place was still the master's commune while it really was a business built around the teachings of the deceased Osho. Without his guidance to surrender to, this place wasn't the same. I imagine that those who joined cults like Jonestown probably had more clarity than I was faced with, but sometimes we all have to do what we need to do in order to take responsibility for ourselves. And so I paused before answering Leelaq, to consider absorbing the risk, and differentiate between what was real and what was not.

Chapter Two

Still sleepy at 6am, I crossed a moat to ascend a staircase leading into a colossal black pyramid that looked like it might blast off into the sky. Inside, I found Jedis in black gowns and white sashes making sure that everyone was sufficiently spaced out across the marbled hall. And then the eerie music began.

To the din of my rasping breath, I used my arms to pump gallons of air into me. I didn't float away as I was pushing it out faster than I took it in. After a monumental effort, a cloud of oxygen billowed within me and created just the right milieu. This was the first stage, and it blew the top off my head to release the genie that had been pulling my strings all my life. Gong!

Like me, my subconscious wasn't a morning person. All hell broke loose. He jumped, screamed, laughed, wept, rolled on the floor and leapt up again like a lunatic. Oddly, there was nothing strange about this. These were ordinary human experiences that had gotten bottled-up inside me for so long that I had forgotten they were there. Gong!

Hoo! Hoo! …No, it wasn't an owl. It was the third stage. Up and down I hopped, chanting the ancient Sufi manta that an Arabic master once taught me was the name of God without any grammatical reference to gender. Because I had purged some of the emotions stuck within, I was lighter, and could jump higher than ever before. Each time I landed, my heels hammered harder into the marble, to which my genie whispered that I should stop lest I hurt myself. Before he could convince me though…Gong!

I froze. I became the statue of my last attempt to jump, too tired to even blink. The exhaustion from all the hopping and shouting created a vacuum inside of me, and I couldn't resist being carried away by a wave of silence. When it crashed, all the confusion that my inner genie could muster up was washed away. Gong!

I spontaneously fell into a dance, like the petals of a flower that push themselves out of the bud. This was the last stage, after which I emerged from the pyramid with my genie put back into his bottle. His hidden-hand was somehow weaker. Down the stairs I descended and by the time I floated across the moat, the cloud of sleep had cleared. I was wide awake...Gong!

Osho's *Dynamic Meditation* is not for the feint-hearted. In the early days of the movement, sannyasins used to do it on the beaches of Bombay, and their public display of emotions caused quite an uproar. In his book *Meditation: The First and Last Freedom*, Osho explains that its design uses the breath to create an alchemical change within the body, which releases life energy that has gotten stuck. It's like having a mental bath, and with some weight thrown off your shoulders, you emerge clearer to face the day. You can Google scientific reports on its benefits and caveats, though the spiritual basis for its design is far more interesting as it sheds some light as to what the ego really is.

I like to think of it as an ever-evolving collage of all your likes and dislikes but, outrageous as always, Osho said that is was nothing.

In a talk entitled *The Fish in the Sea is not Thirsty*, he said that the common wisdom of sacrificing our egos in order to be purer was impossible because the ego was nothing more than an idea. We give reality to it by believing in it. Withdraw support for the idea and the reality disappears. The ego is a substitute personality for our true identities that arises in the absence of self-knowledge.

For instance, people typically define themselves by their talents, values or culture, when asked who they are. While it's useful to think in terms of roles, those ideas we have about ourselves are just that, and not who we are. Identifying with thought is a mistake that is endemic to the west because we subscribe to Descartes's idea that 'we think so we therefore are'. It implies that thought is our identity, and that our minds are exclusively thought.

In a conversation with esteemed Indian businesswoman Vinita Bali however, Sadhguru explains that thought enjoys an importance in western culture only because **Europeans** were subjugated by rigid religious ideas for centuries. When times changed, the freedom to think was a way to celebrate.

He also explained that the English word 'mind' is a rather generic term that fails to convey what our minds actually are. In the yogic sciences the mind has many dimensions, including memory upon which our intellect acts to produce imagination. An intellect that is entirely dependent on what has been committed to memory though is rather limited, and such a mind is incapable of originality. It can only rehash what has been learnt. The yogic culture doesn't believe that our brains are our minds either. The intellect is part of a mental body that has four fundamental parts, and uses every cell in our physical bodies as a vast storage mechanism for memories. Everything, including the blueprint for your great-granny's nose is stored within us, which is how it ends up on your face several generations later.

Another popular example that Sadhguru uses to distinguish between mind and ourselves is how we didn't have bodies upon conception. Nourishment in the womb was used to grow one and, after we were born, a higher intelligence continued working to transform the food we consumed into the bodies we inhabit today. Similarly, your mind is yours, but is not you. You acquired one from living and learning, but to believe that we are the boundary created by the likes and dislikes of our minds is the equivalent of setting aside the higher intelligence that turns seeds into trees and food into you. Wherever we feel constricted in life then is a result of being casualties of our own intellect.

Indeed, witnessing the craziness that oozed out of me during Dynamic Mediation was alarming. It showed that I had been living for quite some time, but knew not a damn thing about myself. More familiar is the intoxicating fantasy we call ourselves…

One evening, a proverbial Shah Rukh Khan arrived at the Shisha Lounge on Pune's 'Riviera' looking cool in a T-shirt and jeans. The jazz band and candlelight intensified his spell over the girls, one in particular clamping her jaw shut when she failed to control her giggles. Let's call her Aishwariya Rai and pretend that pushing her bangs behind her ear wasn't designed to get his attention.

Chicken Boti, naan and Bira ensued, but food can nourish only the body, and not the soul. Shah Rukh leapt to his feet and jumped onto the table. Pouting his lips and squinting his eyes, he sported a look that would've made Derek Zoolander jealous. He then burst into a Bollywood melody, and us guys followed suit as the horny quartet who echoed his every word.

Aishwariya hid coyly behind her shawl. Her entourage of chaste friends played musical chairs around her to rebuff the bold Shah Rukh as nothing more than a player, but he was too handsome, and they all wished they were sitting in Aishwariya's place. That cracked open her shell, and Aishwariya spun out of her sari. She took the hand that Shah Rukh offered and allowed herself to be pulled onto the table, into his arms. They gazed dreamily at each other while the girls kicked off their shoes and bounced upon their mehndi-coloured feet.

Together we all danced around each other, never touching, but never too far apart. The electricity between us was louder than the strumming band.

The dinner ended early for Carla and I, as we were expected at the Welcome Centre the next morning.

While negotiating a rickshaw ride back to the ashram, the rest of the gang packed themselves into a cab destined for a disco. Shah Rukh's head popped out of the window to ask if Aishwariya was joining them. She stopped short of climbing into our rickshaw. She was flustered, perhaps on account of one too many Bira, but more likely gushing at the invitation.

Decisions, decisions!

The next day, Aishwariya was puffing furiously away in the *Smoking Temple*. Yes, even killing yourself has a holy name in the ashram. As expected, things got randy between herself and Shah Rukh the night before, but all she got was the cold shoulder in the morning thereafter. According to 'girl-code', Carla lent an ear in support, and confirmed that it didn't seem like Aishwariya had any unrealistic expectations of her midnight tryst. But that didn't stop Aishwariya from fuming like a dragon.

In the absence of an explanation, I suggested lunch.

Down the road at the *Buddha Paradise* restaurant, the Buddhist chant 'da-da-dumm…da-da-daaaa-dumm' kept droning rhythmically on while the girls invented punishments appropriate for childish men. I ordered a thali and turned my attention to the restaurant's cat who always knew when food was coming. He sauntered over to my feet and meowed that there was once a pirate who walked into a bar…

"What happened to you?" the barman asked, seeing the pirate with a hook for a hand. It turned out that a skirmish with a rival gang got particularly nasty.

"Well, what about that patch on your eye?" the barman enquired, and was in disbelief when the pirate told him that a bird pooped into it one day when looking up to the sky.

"Erm, it was the first day I had the hook on!" the pirate grimaced.

Suffering comes from what we are unconscious of, so Carla noted that the ashram wasn't an environment in which men were encouraged to take responsibility. If you looked at pictures from the commune's heyday, it's almost certain you'd find a few of people lounging around naked. Sexual freedom has always been a part of the commune's DNA, and only recently have they stopped administering Aids tests for visitors. Carla sympathised with the experience Aishwariya had with Shah Rukh, but suggested that it was probably better to let it go.

Aishwariya couldn't. To her, this was a far more insidious problem. Shah Rukh stone-walling her wasn't just keeping her at a distance to avoid the responsibility of one drunken night. It was a form of control, designed to keep her guessing so that she would lay off and not spoil his chances with other women. It hit a nerve because it surreptitiously masked an expectation that she obliged him and, being Indian, Aishwariya loathed expectations.

Arranged marriages are a part of her culture so she was often introduced to men by her family with the intent to marry her off. Against her will, she would have to adorn herself like a prize and parade in front of would-be suitors in the hope of earning their approval. She felt it a demeaning exercise, and argued that love was mutual respect, revealing herself as a woman who preferred a more equitable view of relationships.

Some purring interrupted, and I laid a spoonful of rice on the floor for the cat, wondering how that little creature had learnt to live peacefully while we, with all the sophistication of intellect, still struggled. It reminded me of an incident.

While supporting a friend once, I was waiting in the back of a divorce court where I met a woman who told me that unwritten rules played out in relationships all the time. Putting a ring on someone's finger is tantamount to owning them. Suddenly they become answerable to you, and your needs are beholden to them. That defines the basic contract of having each other to service their respective psychological, emotional and physical needs. It made a possession of her, which she felt was ugly, and her relationship-as-a-transaction left her feeling bitter at someone whom she had loved for many years.

I suppose it was the same bitterness that drove Aishwariya to consider making everyone aware of the game that Shah Rukh was playing. Spreading the news was a formidable way to destroy his chances with the other women and force a confrontation in which she could elicit an explanation from him.

The conversation suddenly paused when Carla looked at her watch. She stood up immediately and warned that we only had 10 minutes to get back to the Welcome Centre. She hated being late and left when I teased that independent women don't satisfy the expectations of others. The little kitty though was delighted that I stayed to finish my gulab jamon, and got a slice of the tasty cinnamon ball drenched in syrup.

A few minutes later, I strolled back with Aishwariya, who enquired about a man's perspective. While dodging cars, trucks, bikes, pedestrians and dogs to cross North Main Road, I tried to be as diplomatic as possible. I pointed out that if she truly believed in equality, then granting Shah Rukh the freedom to make his own choices, for better or worse, was also mutual respect.

"Do you think I earned his behaviour in some way?" she asked when we reached the opposite pavement. Hmm, that was a distinct shift in her mind. I didn't know what happened between them, but I also didn't hesitate to invite her to my room that night to test if she had.

"Only after a few Bira," she winked, her usually bubbly self again. Her strong belief in equality seemed to have waned its grip.

I thought about it thereafter while being bored to death in the Welcome Centre. It was absurd to blame herself for his behaviour but, intending to resolve the situation with Shah Rukh peacefully, yet planning to accomplish that by ambushing him, seemed to be an attempt at levelling the playing field. I guess that was another version of equality, but it was also how Aishwariya's ideals had unwittingly cast a shadow of doubt upon herself. Asking if she had earned his behaviour sounded a lot like guilt for not living up to her own standards.

And that's the game the ego plays.

It wants us to be someone else, usually the person that is agreeable to others. What we see as agreeable though is defined by our ideals, which are nothing more than ideas that we've learnt and now hold in some esteem. And living by ideas that don't belong to us inevitably leaves us asking why we are not the people that we intend to be?

If anything, that was the one question I found hidden behind the personal quest's of almost everyone I met at the ashram. Some thought they were deficient in some way, while others claimed that the world didn't understand them, but lurking in their backstories was always the notion that they were someone other than what the results of their lives illustrated.

It was an interesting question too since having the power of intention implies the ability to act so, indeed, why weren't we the people we intended to be?

Boo! I crept up behind Sandip who was deciding whether to fix the paper jam in the printer. Only the ashram's techies were allowed to fiddle with the equipment, but a guest was waiting on him, and Sandip was staring at the disobedient printer with disdain. Now, in those early days of WAM, newbies like me were warned to merely observe without exercising any initiative. Protocol was so important in the Welcome Centre that we were made to wait until someone decided when we were ready for actual work. The work wasn't rocket science either so I was bored stiff and volunteered to break the rules and fix the printer.

Sandip frowned. He's a disciplined yogi who doesn't indulge in sweets and chocolates as he says, "it's not goot forrr botty". I can only imagine what he thought of us violating the rules.

Generally, in life, us humans are only
doing three things: Earning a living, procreating, and coming to terms with the fact that death is inevitable.

Success is the ideal that drives survival, marriage the one that elevates procreation, and meaning is where we draw our self-worth from in the face of death. Everyone is free to choose where the ideals to resolve each of those quests come from, but the mental model can always be summed up as a worthy ideal with a set of corresponding behaviours to attain it. That's the beauty of your mind. You can aim it at anything you desire, and it will act accordingly.

Taking responsibility is another matter altogether, and I was an expert in recklessness. I reminded Sandip that he didn't have the luxury of deliberating. A quick glance at the irate guest proved me right, and Sandip stepped aside to take advantage of my insolence for the few minutes it took to fix the printer. It must've been a **relief actually, as** he also asked me to teach him how to schedule emails so that he could send his daily reports way after he was done for the day.

Those and other office tricks soon made me a sort of handyman for the Welcome Centre. I wasn't ever bored again because shifting ideals are not rare.

For instance, a Muslim friend once told me that in Islam, husbands are allowed four wives. The privilege of polygamy terrified him though because it was also a husband's duty to be the sole breadwinner of the family, and he would have to work four times as hard.

"So, what the Imams are effectively saying is that you can only look lasciviously at the other three?" I asked.

My doubts aside, the ideals we adopt for ourselves are useful to structure our lives. Books like *'The Secret'* employ the method of repetition in order to affirm new ideas in our heads from which our actions can follow. Self-hypnotism goes a step further toward mind management by engaging the emotions and associating them to physical sensations. For example, you can project all the disgust you have onto your fist then, the next time you're offered a slice of delectable chocolate cake, you can simply clench your fingers to trigger the repulsion again. In that way you can maintain your weight. Visualisation meditations like 'Chit Shakti' go even further by using your imagination to create mental and emotional intensity for a particular objective. Once you aim your mind, your actions follow in order to manifest a desired outcome because the premise upon which all of this works is that your thoughts create your world.

So, these are all powerful methods to organise our lives. They empower us to facilitate great changes as conscious **choices combat** the tendency for our lives to unfold accidentally. Not taking the time to organise it was precisely why everyone in WAM found the Welcome Centre toxic.

When I arrived there a few days later, a maroon-robe shouted "Shiva!" from the back office. In his customary gentle manner, Shiva namaste'd to the guests he was registering and slid away to ensure that documents were being filed correctly. "Shiva!" someone else shouted a moment later. He popped out of the back office, and ran over to the cashier. While still there, "Shiva!" echoed through the Welcome Centre again. A little later, Shiva returned to his guests at the registration desk, this time however sans the kind Namaste.

The Welcome Centre devolved into this chaos as a result of the coordinator leaving abruptly. The gossip at the fishpond was that she was given a talking to on behalf of the staff who found her bossy, but the intervention with the powers that be in Lao Tzu House didn't end too well. Luckily, Shiva and the other staff shared the sentiment of giving every guest at the ashram a welcome as warm as their own reverence for Osho. Their devotion, however, was only a plaster for the lack of efficiency at the WC. I call the Welcome Centre that as the acronym WC also means Water Closet, or toilet.

Common problems in the workplace, I guess, is why Osho referred to work as "group therapy". Working in the commune is a compulsory part of WAM as engaging others provides an opportunity to remain meditative during unpredictable daily activities. When it doesn't affect you that much, you perform better. Professional athletes have consistently corroborated this notion when describing the zone they tap into when playing their sports. It's a state of being that's so wholly engaged in an activity that time itself disappears. Osho called it the skill of 'totality', and WAM is structured to cultivate it as a means to unite the split between work and play.

To Osho, an activity was simply activity when it didn't have any specific motivation behind it. You were free to enjoy anything you chose to do when you didn't split yourself by utilitarian notions.

The staff at the WC, however, were not employees. They were devotees who came to the ashram for their own personal growth and weren't really interested in organisational objectives like productivity or efficiency. After all, WAM was a programme that we all paid for so, really, all of us working in it were customers ourselves – and that is a conflict of interest that reflects a much deeper contradiction in spirituality today.

To put it into context, understand that the Welcome Centre was historically located alongside a sign that read 'The Gateless Gate'. It's a Zen paradox used by ancient masters to point seekers to the present moment where they said that liberation could be found. Back in the day, a short but energetic woman called Laxmi, who served as Rajneesh's first personal secretary, ran the whole commune from it. But when money became a problem, the infamous Ma Anand Sheela suggested that the commune borrow money from its members, and the overwhelming level of contributions that followed inspired the establishment of the ashram's very profitable bank. Sheela went on to become Rajneesh's next secretary, and wrote in her book about life with him that their then estimated $60-millon business was based on meditation as a product.

Fast-forward to today, a world in which priests have lost the privilege to dispense spiritual advice to a 'Netflix-generation of spirituality' who choose what they want to see, believe or practise. Meditation is no longer an obscure practice of those who opted for lifelong tutelage by a saint wearing a napkin in some Himalayan cave. Today, it is rapidly gaining traction as a practical means to take charge of your life.

I suppose religion's death is imminent, as why would anyone need a God when they can get the lives that they want by themselves?

This is especially true if you paid attention to how meditation is flaunted in popular media. It's easy to get the impression that it's a kind of superpower. Words like 'genius', 'legend' and 'hero' are used to characterise it, and indicate the power to craft your destiny in the same way that priests claim praying to God will deliver the life you want. Whether either works or not is beside the point. Simply recognise how interchangeably the marketing is with divinity.

It's as if God has reincarnated into an entrepreneur.

And any businessman can see that the need for meditation during the Rajneeshee movement back in the sixties is very much the same as the need for it today, as humans still have four limbs and a mind. In fact, in a 'Netflix-generation of spirituality', the demand for meditation is more intense because it adds to the number of available product choices.

Technology has made variety commonplace in our world, but focussing exclusively on choice raises the question as to which methods are authentic ways to grow as opposed to those which have unwittingly made us sheep for financial slaughter.

Back in Rajneesh's days, his devotees were essentially in a co-op with him. They're called 'sannyasins', and were building a self-sustainable commune for themselves to live in alongside their master. The ashram today though is a business built around

Rajneesh's teachings, and devotees don't have a communal share in the institution as they once had when their guru was alive.

Some critics have voiced strong opinions against the Osho International Foundation (OIF) for this approach, and I suppose they're justified, as Osho's teachings can't be divorced from an institution built around him. But it's also fair to allow the OIF the commercial means to continue spreading their master's word in a self-sustainable way. Also, they were apparently instructed to do so by Rajneesh himself on his deathbed. Though all this may be a bitter pill to swallow for the sannyasin community, that controversy is not a concern here.

Instead, for ordinary people like you and me, who are just looking for some joy in our lives, it's becoming increasingly important to distinguish the noise created by spiritual entrepreneurs from authentic spiritual practises.

Diving into that subject, I found that methods like affirmations or self-hypnotism described earlier may be effective to achieve an outcome, but they don't really transform your life. Those methods still operate on the level of the 'Body-Mind', which constitutes your physical body and its associated thoughts and emotions. That perspective on life is centred around what mystics refer to as desires. They are the building blocks of a false personality like the ego because what you like, or want, comes from what you perceive you lack as a person. It's drastically different from a higher perspective like enlightenment that was being taught by Osho and other mystics.

A simple way to understand the difference is to ask yourself where the life within you is really coming from?

Those who hold the title of being awakened teach methods to evolve beyond the mind, and access the realm of spirit, which they say is the source of everything in existence. All that is born comes from it and goes back there after death. It has nothing to do with the practical human needs for survival or the ambitions to be rich, pretty, or cool. Evolving requires a leap, just as fish grew lungs when they became amphibians. That's what meditation helps you with, which is significant because it gives you an understanding that your needs are only **relatively important in the grander scheme of things.**

Many courses labelled as 'spiritual' don't really teach that though, and similarly, all was not what it seemed in the Welcome Centre either.

There was a method to everyone's madness that was roughly based on a set of policies instituted by Lao Tzu House, the administrative head of the **commune. They asked me** to complete an instructional video that taught the WC's operating standards to the staff. A previous video existed, but was flawed with procedural inaccuracies, so I undertook the mission armed with the Welcome Centre's bible – the 'Staff Manual'.

Natalia took one look at it, threw her pretty hair over her shoulders and tossed the damned thing right back into the drawer from whence it came. I understood why when flipping through it. There were pages of single-spaced lists, each bearing instructions that were broken down to the most granular of details, and then repeated ad infinitum with such minute changes that they could only be detected under intense scrutiny. Apart from having the power to put Snow White back to sleep, it took an aeon to make any sense of it.

A couple of frustrated days later, I discovered much more than the instructions to operate the WC's software and file its documentation hidden between the lines.

One page listed twenty-odd countries from which visitors were considered a security risk. They were to be screened by the security chief before being admitted to the ashram. Mohammed, an Arab guest, quizzed me about the necessity of such an intrusive interrogation, and I suspect it was a concern that he only shared with me because I have a Middle Eastern name too. I didn't tell him that the interrogation was just the beginning of a methodical way to control movements within the ashram.

For instance, there are flags used to identify disruptive people. The letter 'P' labelled those alleged to have come to the ashram for sex as 'perverts', and it was policy to assume that 'browner-skinned' people were leering sexual maniacs. For them it was compulsory to attend an informal talk on how to behave respectably toward Western women. There was also the 'S' flag which was used for people who suffered from holier-than-thou dispositions, and annoyed other meditators with their constant pontificating.

Such were the methods used to enforce obedience at the ashram and they didn't amount to what should be a standard procedural manual at all. After some study, it proved to be a window into the governance policies of the entire Osho establishment. It aimed to capture a vast amount of detail about those who visited the ashram, and the many questions posed during the 30-minute registration process made most people ask how their personal details were used.

Unofficially I was told that they were used to maintain the meditative environment that Osho said was all people really needed to grow, and the ashram-elder who told me that beamed the knowing smile of a secret fellowship that decided the fate of the meditators. She may have even been a member of the council that ran the ashram as I sensed that she had the power to banish me at will – as callously as the council exiled some of its own members when disagreements arose after Osho's death. Those who were left behind behaved as a tightly-knit family unit who had lived and grown together and, watching them sometimes, it was easy to understand why people addressed each other as 'Dearly Beloved'. They had such a strong sense of belonging that it had me wondering where my place in this life was. I was moved, and so I put my back into my duties at the Welcome Centre.

I decided to leave the place better than I found it, as it was the only way to tell whether I was just seeing what I wanted to see and telling myself the story that I wanted to hear.

Chapter Three

Bupendra and I looked curiously at each other when a loud moan came from behind the curtain. The man from Vietnam stumbled out of the change room with his head stuck within the trunk of a maroon robe. His arms were tangled half-way into the sleeves, the loose ends of which another old geyser began tugging at. The geyser was travelling with the man from Vietnam, and together the old friends caused quite a ruckus while wrestling with each other. Bupendra and I stepped back, grinning.

The curtain to the other change room was suddenly thrown aside. A younger man leapt out of it and slid across the floor on his socks. He was chaperoning the two pensioners on their trip to India, and it was plain to see that he couldn't handle them even if he didn't try so hard. He pulled the old geyser away from the man from Vietnam and began untangling his father from the robe.

The geyser jumped back to my side and showed me that a finger was missing from his hand.

"Grr!" he said. "Grrrrr!" he exclaimed again when realising that I didn't get it.

After a lengthy explanation in a language that I didn't understand, I discovered that the geyser lost his finger while operating a saw, and now his hand was too weak to help the man from Vietnam. Luckily, the young son managed to pry the robe off, and there it was, the same infectious grin the man from Vietnam had when first arriving at the Welcome Centre.

His entrance was unmissable. He threw his arms up and gasped as if he'd just seen Jesus. He then took his friend by the hand and waltzed over to the waterfall, where he poked a finger into it to demonstrate that it was real water.

"My God!"

Following the dramatic exclamation, the pair promptly struck a pose for their picture to be taken. A maroon-robe quickly ran over, yelling that no photographs were allowed in the ashram.

"No pictures?" the geyser without a finger moaned in disappointment.

"No pictures!" the young son yelled back in disbelief.

The man from Vietnam simply nodded and said "Okay!", then turned to talk to the fish in the pond. With his lips pouted and cheeks sucked all the way in, I swear the fish seemed to understand him.

A man like him is an oddity in our world. To him, all of life was play, and the spontaneity with which he enjoyed it seemed to be the secret that is often sought after. He reminded me of Osho himself, in his *Star Trek* uniform, namaste'ing at strangers with a huge grin on his face. I tried it myself in front of the bathroom mirror once and lasted only a few minutes before my cheeks became sore. I discovered then that joy wasn't something created. It's a quality that arises by going with the flow. That path, however, is one that passes through a great many dangers, such as discovering that an absence of God, or meaning in life, is as risky as discovering there is one.

What if you don't like what you find?

The man from Vietnam was happy to allow life to unfold as it would. I later learnt from his son that he had saved a portion of his pension, probably for decades, to afford the trip to India. He simply wanted to offer gratitude to the master in lieu of lessons learnt though, after paying double the price for robes and having to shell out more cash to keep their knapsacks in a locker while roaming the campus that forbade bags, his son thought the whole meditation resort experience was a huge rip-off. The man from Vietnam produced the money anyway and urged his son to pay whatever was necessary. It was important to him to carry out his intentions sincerely, even while his offspring scolded him for being childish and irresponsible.

I however was rather inspired by the spectacle. The man from Vietnam had a spectacular trust in life while I still deliberated my place in it.

He was in a category of guests to the ashram that I referred to as 'fans'. Another was 'sannyasins', or Rajneesh's devotees who had likely participated in building the commune too. They were usually older, and in the minority compared to the younger demographic who frequent the ashram today. Youthful interests were mainly focussed on the meditative activities that could help solve their career, relationship or personal problems, and so I thought of them as 'meditators'. They were easily differentiated from the 'spiritually-curious', who walked willy-nilly into the Welcome Centre, and were attracted to the ashram's notoriety.

I began paying attention to those little details after being teamed up with a diplomatic Argentinian called Sheela – not to be confused with the infamous Ma Anand Sheela who once ran the commune. In the austere surroundings of Lao Tzu House, Sheela expressed concern over a report listing arrivals at the WC.

Upon inspection, I found that the report was useful to those who prepared accommodations at the campus guesthouses, the 'multiversity' as to its occupancy rate, and of course whether the fees collected eventually tallied up with the bottom line in the financial report. While Sheela herself was only using the report to facilitate the 'Welcome Morning', it was clear that the inaccuracies had a wide impact.

"This data is being captured in the WC..." she explained, not having to say anything more. Lingering unspoken in the ether between us was the Welcome Centre's reputation as the armpit of the ashram.

"I'll just have to whip them!" I mused about the follies my colleagues and I were perpetrating, but Lao Tzu House remained as quiet as the meditation hall. Sheela too gathered the leaves of her report sans a grin even. I guess, she and I both knew that supervision wasn't optional at the ashram.

Welcome Morning is the compulsory induction course that lays down the commune's rules - its culture, so to speak. It's meant to teach meditation, but also tells people how to dress, behave, and eat in the ashram, which was why many who attend the session come out despising it. In one session that I helped facilitate, a guy shook like he was possessed by the devil during Kundalini Meditation. He then ignored my assistance to complain about being forced to spend half of his one-day visit to the ashram in Welcome Morning. Needless to say, the session wasn't always effective. When guests groaned at being automatically enrolled for it during registration, I sold Welcome Morning as a 'free' course just to watch their faces light up, and then quiz them about it later.

Others in WAM mocked it enthusiastically too.

The Welcome Morning jingle was sung by a short Asian woman alongside a tall Caucasian one that tapped her foot like it was a Tourette's reaction. My friends in WAM would monkey her sometimes, when commune laws like the prohibition of mobile phones, or the injunction against jumpers that weren't maroon, was too strictly enforced.

"Wel-come to the Awe-sho Inter-national Meditation…Rrr-esort!" they jeered one evening while waiting for a cab. A pedestrian stepped away from us hastily, but nothing could stop us WAMmers from voicing our dissatisfaction with authority. It emphasised the irony of conditioning the behaviour of people who came to the ashram because Osho promised a way out of the harmful conditioning our own societies imposed upon us.

The rebelliousness was fun, though I spent the cab ride staring out the window at the throngs of Indians who all seemed determined to be going somewhere and doing something. It struck me just how difficult it was to live as carefree as the man from Vietnam.

Think of a billboard ad that reads 'Just Do It!' alongside the picture of Tiger Woods swinging a golf club. The logic follows that a set of clubs that matches his brand will improve your game to a professional level but, if you buy into that, you're not buying a set of golf clubs anymore. Your money is being spent on an emotional experience that you're hoping to acquire by modelling Tiger's success. It's an invitation to the championship lifestyle that he represents. Only when those clubs end up on a dusty shelf in the garage some time later, does it become apparent that they can't ever be a substitute for the years of golfing practise Tiger has had. The logic, you then see, is flawed. More importantly, the logic was used to justify an emotional experience you wanted, recognition in this case.

Now no baby is born ambitious, so our emotional responses are often learnt behaviour.

This was addressed in a YouTube video in which Osho's decision to put a price tag on meditations was challenged. Osho explained that the value of 'free' is nothing in a world that appreciates only the things they've achieved. We live in a goal-orientated culture, he said, so a viable strategy to free humanity from cultural conditioning was to make people earn their liberation.

And why not? Last I checked, personal development was an industry in which only 7% of the customers use the products they paid 100% for.

The instant gratification implied in that trivia reflects the urgency that we feel within to be doing something, or going somewhere. #FOMO is the social media hashtag that proves how popular that anxiety really is, but keeping busy, doesn't answer the question as to what you're actually doing. Would self-improvement even be an industry if we were simply aware of that? I imagine that's why people never stepped out of line at the ashram either. Annoying as Welcome Morning was, many people still need someone to tell then what to do with themselves.

Some say it's the ghost of our education system which fills us up with information solely for the purpose of becoming productive members of society. In his talk *The Golden Gate*, Osho says that this preoccupation we have with survival is a deep and unconscious conditioning that comes from the many centuries of man's struggle with life. We are now fixated on it, and life has become just a struggle to survive. Scientists have made it more convincing too, he says, with the theory of 'survival of the fittest', which has encouraged man to become invulnerable citadels instead of open and alive human beings.

This is really something to think about as we define freedom as the ability to live life on our own terms when those very terms are ideas we've been conditioned to want. Freedom isn't the problem, yet. Our unconscious choices are.

Mrs. Friedman was shocked when her dentist told her that he needed to extract her tooth. "I'd rather have a baby!" she replied, to which the dentist retorted, "well, would you make up your mind, so I know how to adjust the chair?"

The shopkeeper too sighed as he waited for me to make up my mind. There was a line of cereal boxes on the counter between us, which I was inspecting to see how the same brands are localised around the world. The variances gave me an insight into a culture in the same way that the infamous 'McDonalds Test' compares the prices of Big-Mac's around the globe to indicate the standard of living in various places. Chacha, the shopkeeper, found it odd that I made a point of visiting supermarkets on my travels to understand the aspirations of the locals.

"Life isn't an academic question," he argued, pointing to the family of beggars living on the pavement outside.

His theory was that skilled Indian labour was colonising the western world today as eagerly as India was invaded by the British centuries ago because it was a solution to a practical problem. Chacha too was taught to be a pragmatist by poverty. He told me how he had to apply a generous helping of elbow grease to claw his way out of the gutter and earn the little supermarket we were standing in. It still demanded extremely long working hours out of him.

"Life is not for sissies!" he added for effect.

The guy had a point. While exploring the many subcultures of spirituality, I've come across people whose lives were ruled by the stars, spells, smudge-sticks and psychedelic experiences. Everything seems to have a cosmic significance in the realm of aspirations, but the outsourcing of happiness to any divine idea rarely improves anyone's lives - even those who know what the devil 'Mercury being in retrograde' actually **means.** When that phrase trended on Facebook, it was a highfalutin way of blaming the cosmos for our lives not going as planned, and I like to think of it as a perfect example of why Facebook is celebrity in a middle-class skin.

A simple glance at your Facebook timeline will reveal what people find important, entertaining or useful. What they choose to share reflects who they are, as it makes subconscious statements such as "this is what I'm about". It's the equivalent of associating themselves with what they hold in some esteem, and that's a form of curated personality that celebrity is. Social media then, as the uber-efficient agent of impressions, is largely a giant ambition machine for those who aspire, and aspiration is mostly a middle-class trait. It's the digital age manifestation of the American dream, which still translates into a comfortable life with social power.

"So, you want to 'make it'?" I asked. I knew that Chacha was really advocating some common sense, but I was tempted to play with him.

I dared to point out that his pragmatism was aspirational too. There was nothing wrong with having the things we need but, I challenged him, a purely materialistic view of life reduced him to a creature of need.

"That too is missing out on a quality of life," I added for effect.

Using his middle finger, Chacha pushed his spectacles up to the bridge of his nose and laughed.

"Arre yaar!" he exclaimed, throwing his hands up. What he meant was that millions of people were creating a better life by working harder so who was I to be rebellious about it?

Hmph! I smirked. If it weren't for rebels challenging the status quo we would scarcely see the folly of our ways. I was still playing with him, but maybe I went too far by pointing to the family of beggars living on the street outside and saying: "That *is* an academic question!"

Except for the one in my hand, Chacha packed away the other cereal boxes on the shelf behind him. He turned around again to inspect my robes suspiciously.

"Accha, so you are looking for yourself?"

That's when I knew I should've rather shut my mouth. He grinned when I told him that the ashram wasn't just a cosy womb I had escaped to. I was working there too, but there it was, the shame that must be endured when pursuing our own wellbeing instead of what's expected of us.

Chacha had no idea that meditation wasn't used as an attempt to find ourselves. Often, what people call 'seeking' only literally translates to a search. That meaning could likely have come from religious thinking, which supposes the idea of a god, and then attempts to prove it through a search for evidence. But no matter how convincing a logic you find, the truth about God is simply that we don't know. We may believe in one, but subscribing to an idea is not a knowing.

Eckhart Tolle is quoted as saying that the great obstacle for spiritual seekers is that they're searching for 'some thing', so a better definition of the inner groping we all go through to find ourselves is the acknowledgement that you know, you don't know why your life is unfolding haphazardly, and want to know. This is how Sadhguru defined seeking and goes on to say that "[seeking] means that no matter what Krishna or Shiva said, you have to know the truth in your own experience".

Looking outwardly for ourselves equates to the experience that people refer to as feeling 'lost', whereas all that is necessary is to simply turn inwards, towards where you already are. That's what meditation is a tool for.

Osho's view was that we have never really been accepted for who we are from the time we were children. Our societies have always tried to guide and improve us, and while they may have meant well, constantly being conditioned to believe ourselves as being wrong led to us feeling that we are somehow not enough. The origins of rebelliousness are then easy to see, but why get distracted by trying to prove a point?

George Bernard Shaw's words are profound.
He says that life isn't about finding ourselves. It's about creating ourselves.

In any case, I considered myself lucky to have been insulted by Chacha, as my perspective on life wasn't formulated out of an exposure to the grand scale of poverty that he had grown up in. I gave Chacha my rupees and left with a box of Honey Loops to chomp on the way back to the ashram. As a devotee of the e-Guru, Google Maps, I never had to seek in the outside world.

Back at the ashram, I skipped past the Welcome Centre, down the white-pebbled path, and into Radha

Hall. I was attending a course there called Inner Skills as a part of WAM. Like all things Osho, it began with some dancing.

Sadhana, the facilitator, **then began** evolving our communication skills. Her theory was that employing facts in a discussion was a result of communicating using the mind, while expressing feelings came from the heart. She wanted to teach us how to express ourselves from the belly, which is the base of your very being. She said it was a holistic, and more effective **way, to** conduct daily activities.

The seat of your being in Zen is located about an inch below your belly button. It's an energy centre called the 'Hara', which yogis describe as the power-inlet through which spirit flows into the body. From there, energy is distributed along the masculine and feminine channels, and the entire human physiology is connected to the breath, **which regulates the** thoughts and emotions that ultimately shape the results of our lives. It's a fascinating view of being human as it explains how we are intimately connected to the universe.

In his book *'Mystics Musings'*, Sadhguru explains that the Earth's equator is divided into 360 degrees, and each degree comprises of 60 minutes. One minute equates to a single nautical mile, so the circumference of the earth at the equator is 21,600 nautical miles. Now, on average, we take approximately 15 breaths per minute, which tallies up to 900 breaths an hour, or 21,600 breaths every day. It's not a coincidence that your breath is in alignment with the rotation of the Earth, which itself is a cog in the larger machine of the solar system. Once aligned with the greater mechanism of nature, you effectively communicate with it, and your wellbeing is then a natural consequence.

To demonstrate the method of communicating holistically, Sadhana flung out the legs of a pair of pants, maroon of course, and offered it to Alexandra to buy. It was a common scenario that everyone could relate to, and Alexandra pretended that the pair of pants was both the right size and style that would suit her. But she refused to buy them as she was in disbelief. Who buys anything simply because it is offered?

Alexandra took them from Sadhana, and became suddenly animated as if conducting a Zig Ziegler seminar. By the end of it, we were convinced that those pants were exactly what we needed to gain access to all the interesting activities on campus. Seeing them as a possibility, rather than the maroon pair of pants that they were, had us itching to spend our money. It was then that we discovered that Alexandra was a seasoned saleswoman, and experience had taught her that the direct communication style Sadhana was proposing would only be rejected in ordinary life.

Everyone else nodded, for they knew that was just how the world worked.

We got talking about our jobs, and how a certain amount of tact was required to get things done. Almost everyone had acquired masks of politeness or diplomacy in order to go with the flow of their lives. It was far easier than trying to communicate meticulously. Sadhana quickly switched to a video of Osho, and no one bothered asking if he was qualified to answer their questions either.

Whether that too was a mask is an interesting question as the purpose of wearing them, according to Osho, is power. He said that we only seek power because we have been made to feel inadequate by our societies. It breeds the urge to be better, wealthy or famous as a means to allay our inner fears about ourselves, and the logical end to that idea is desiring the ability to have others do our bidding for us. That is his definition of power, and is what we aspire to when pursuing success. Any vested interest in others though, Osho considered as a form of trampling over our brethren, but that's how we're taught to meet our survival needs by the same society who has a vested interest in us.

Come to think of it, it was precisely what Sheela and I were attempting to do in the Welcome Centre. To resolve the errors on her report, we needed the staff to obey due process, or else...

I arrived at the WC the following day to find everyone huddled around the fish pond where the whispers said that Anurag, the new coordinator, was appointed because she moved in powerful circles within the commune. The destruction caused by that gossip summed itself up by the end of the day, when the staff flopped back into the chairs around the pond, tired from being given one instruction by Anurag and another by Shiva. He was certainly the most experienced of us in the WC, but having two captains resulted in disagreements that left the staff even less effective than before.

A single glance would recognise that as ordinary life, but with a costume change to robes and sandals.

I escaped the negative vibes by hiding in the back office where I followed up on the test cases Sheela and I had implemented. I found the usual salutation in the emails contracted to merely 'Beloved', and the content of the messages that followed laced with frustration. Lao Tzu House was losing their patience with us as our test cases were indeed producing results, albeit ones that confused the erroneous data we had to begin with.

According to the yogi's, the reason why we operate blindly is a matter of physiology. Sadhguru explains in a *Satsang* video that all our senses are directed outwardly to perceive the world around us. This results in such misperceptions as life being the billions of bits of information fed to us by our five senses. All that data is layered upon each other to produce a collective package, called an experience, that keeps on miraculously manifesting one moment to the next, from birth to death. But to be alive or dead are merely different states of existence that we are ordinarily unaware of because our physical senses can't comprehend it.

If that sounds like a fantastic claim, there's a popular story in history that says the Native Indians of America never saw the European ships pulling up to the coast until men disembarked. Up till then, they had never seen a ship and, because it was such an alien concept, they failed to see the vessels until they were at their shores.

Our conditioning similarly assumes many of the choices available to us. In the WC it was boiling down to supporting Anurag as the appointed coordinator or rooting for Shiva's experience, but those choices were only relative to the context of management. The staff had their own choices. They could leave, or pretend to be sick. Choices are almost always relative to the context they're made in, which is how our conditioning limits us. We only see what the ideas in our heads allow us to see, and so become polarised from real life. One man's opinions relative to another becomes, on a grander scale, the world as we know it today with all its boons and terrors. It can be summarised as one economy competing with another, or one nation's politics against another, all of which is still a pretty binary view, and why the man from Vietnam is such an anomaly with his many shades of colour.

Cuckoo-Rukoo! The ashram clock crowed a couple days later. It did so on the hour, every hour, even though many people were surprised to discover that it wasn't an enlightened rooster.

I was waiting outside Krishna House, listening to other WAMmers who needed some clarity before dismissing the WAM programme as disappointing. We were funnelled into a room and sat down, after which their confusion multiplied. The question as to how many cells there were in the human body suddenly accosted us.

Five billion! Ten trillion! Two million! Everyone took wild guesses while Amrito stroked his stark-white beard and gave no clues. Then, in dulcet tones, he answered his own question.

Harmony within the human body happened naturally because every cell wasn't fighting to attain its own personal agenda. Nature too works flawlessly because trees functioned as trees, rocks continued to be rocks, and people, themselves. A bushel doesn't pine to be an oak tree as there is an intrinsic dignity in accepting the purpose that nature has given it. Yearning to be something other than what they are is a disease that man acquired, but we know harmony instinctively too as we are also part of nature.

"The key to understanding our place in existence wasn't to seek it," Amrito said, then exclaimed "go for broke!".

Children do that while playing Cowboys and Indians, he explained. The joy in their game erupts spontaneously without any expectations to have fun, and life similarly was more enjoyable if we just let it play out, like the man from Vietnam did.

Existence, Amrito said while recalling Osho's explanation, occurred in ranges that served specific purposes in the cosmic machine that is nature. There are many varieties of grasses, for instance, as there are types of cows which feed on them to produce milk. Where one range of creation stopped, another began, and so all of existence was related to each other through an interdependence that characterises nature as a living organism.

Trying to do something to fit in then was a misunderstanding.

The intellect, as Dr Wayne Dyer explained, is a wonderful tool to understand things, but it works by breaking things down. Slicing up a human being and laying all the parts out will teach you much about the human body, but it won't ever answer where the life within it came from. To discover that you need intelligence, which is a unifying force that's capable of seeing the sum of all parts. If we follow it to the very end, where our perspectives are inclusive of the planet, galaxy, universe and all, then we experience a total unity. In a single word, we call that 'God'.

Suddenly there was context, then POOF! Amrito disappeared.

Outside Krishna House again, the mood was decidedly different. None of the queries they had about WAM were addressed in the meeting but my fellow WAMmers had tossed away all their concerns. They were now intoxicated by a vision far larger than they'd ever imagined.

Krishnamurti, an exceptionally rational man, once described the situation as such that when a man claims to be enlightened, we flock to him to ask how he did it. We rarely question what constitutes his claim, and thereby make ourselves gullible in the hope of fulfilling our own self-serving motivations.

This behaviour is supported by a culture that discourages trusting our own intuitions. For instance, it's a common desire to be a good person, but we don't see it as a function that's intrinsic to our humanity. Instead, being good in our culture is a process of using some moral principle to identify everyone else as bad. By comparison we are good, but that's the logic which is responsible for the many people who are slaughtered while one religion wars with another.

If anything, we subscribe to our pecking orders because they provide a sense of belonging, which is not only a powerful emotional trigger, but also enjoys an importance that we rarely consider.

Imagine yourself surrounded by family, friends, lovers and enemies. There's a hierarchy to those relationships, prioritised by need. For instance, shelter trumps happiness, so your employer enjoys more power over you than your lover does. That hypothetical situation illustrates how, by helping to fulfil each other's needs, power is distributed across a proverbial ladder that we imagine as the hierarchy of society. Measures like money only bestow people with greater esteem because it reflects an ability to meet their needs more readily, while others may still be scavenging to survive. By adopting the values and beliefs of a specific culture, we gain a position on that ladder, and are empowered to navigate the social hierarchy in order to service our personal needs. A sense of belonging then is a practical necessity that's strongly connected to our individual survival. As the old adage says: 'There is strength in numbers.'

Now consider all the pomp and glory we attribute to the idea of success when it's really just a safety mechanism.

Of course, stepping out to challenge the status quo, as Buddha did, also threatens your friends and family who depend on you for their needs – and that, Dearly Beloveds, is why the public beating has not gone out of fashion yet.

A sense of belonging doesn't substitute for a fulfilling life. It can't. Living by the rationale of 'what's good for the goose is good for the gander' is merely a recipe for producing zealots. Zealots don't ever make up their own minds. Their truth is borrowed, and that is the spell of spirituality.

Cuckoo-Rukoo!

Chapter Four

Everyone gasped. We weren't sure if Moritz was joking again, but there he sat in his bright orange Salwar Khameez suit. It was printed over with large golden hands held in 'yoga mudra', the same posture that statues of Buddha hold their fingers in while meditating. The outfit was perfectly ostentatious for Savya Rasa, the posh restaurant we were dining at.

Upon entering, we stepped into a cloud of sweet incense smoke that made the place feel like the decadent brothel featured in the Bollywood classic 'Devdas'. In ancient India, brothels weren't seedy establishments. They were visited upon by kings, who valued the street-smarts that courtesans could impart, and sometimes even sent their progeny there for schooling in the art of life. Like someone who had had graduated from such a university, Moritz was a man who preferred to think for himself.

We were talking about the 'Evening Meeting', also known as the 'White-Robed Brotherhood'. It's a daily meditation at the ashram in which people danced wildly until the music suddenly stopped. Everyone would then throw their arms up and shout 'OSHO!' It's called a 'Stop Exercise', and was invented by Georges Gurdjieff, a Russian mystic who pioneered several techniques to put human beings under intense pressure as a means to squeeze their true selves out. Stop Exercises shocked the mind out of its usual pattern of thinking, and the sudden interruption facilitated a few moments of utter silence within. Osho used it to create the climate in which people could go deeper into the actual meditation that followed the dancing in the Evening Meeting.

Moritz, however, didn't like the idea of shouting out anyone's name during the exercise. Instead, he yelled 'arschloch', which is German for 'arsehole', and when he demonstrated how similar it sounded to Osho's name, he wasn't joking, but we all laughed.

I wished Carla had joined us but she was busy planning a trip to Chiang Mai. Since deciding to extend her stay at the ashram, she had to leave India in order to get her visa renewed upon re-entry.

My present company, however, was delightful. They were the perks of working in the Welcome Centre, where I met pretty much everyone who visited the ashram. The five of us seated at the dining table were really strangers to each other, all visiting the ashram for our own reasons, but in agreement that it was like the *Algonquin* of spirituality, and too unique a place to not discuss.

We had all made a point of visiting the Chuang Tzu auditorium in Osho's old home. The garage doors are made of glass, through which you can see one of the

93 Rolls Royce's that Rajneesh used to drive past sannyasins and wave at them. A carved wooden door leads into the main house from there. Stepping through it is guaranteed to give pause as the home is lined from floor to ceiling in eloquent white bookshelves. The rest of the walls are clad in mirrors, and the passage through the library delivers you to a room with nothing in it but a dental chair. Why it's there is another story altogether but, pass through, and you will arrive at the circular meditation auditorium. Above the double-volume windows which stare into the garden is a chandelier almost as large as the hall itself. From it hangs little crystals that glitter the full spectrum of the rainbow, which makes the place feel less like a spiritual retreat than it does an exotic oriental spa.

"It's too, erm, *Liberace*!" Moritz quipped, scoring another laugh from us. It was an accurate description of the wealth on display that bothered many people.

Earlier that day, I had registered a group of ashram-hoppers who came from Rishikesh. Ours was the umpteenth ashram they had arrived at during their three-month excursion around India, and their first words were an exclamation as to its decadence. Holy people with dots on their heads, and meals taken communally on the floor, was replaced at the Osho ashram by access cards and Rajneesh currency vouchers. It wasn't at all the 'Eat-Pray-Love' experience that they craved. Their asceticism reflected the inclination of many seekers to only give a spiritual solution credit if it was difficult to attain.

A man sat upon the rocks every day, so deep in meditation that even the frogs refrained from croaking. When he finished one afternoon, he climbed down to find the same beggar that watched him meditating every day, still watching him curiously. In all seriousness, he confessed that he wanted nothing more than some relief from the constant stream of thoughts racing through his mind.

"There's just so many of them," he explained to the beggar.

"Why aren't you grateful?" the beggar asked, "you have more than others!"

Asceticism has historically been observed in many religious traditions as a way to become a good person. It is generally characterized by an abstinence from sensual pleasures in order to pursue spiritual goals, though some practices go as far as abandoning personal hygiene, or even self-flagellation. Rajneesh himself was against such morbid practices. To him, life was an occasion to be celebrated, and he supported wealth creation as a means to afford the spiritual quest.

Defenders of Rajneesh say that his excesses of diamond-encrusted watches and a fleet of cars were merely devices used to expose the ridiculousness of materialism, and its mentality of more. Commoditizing the most desirable things was intended to have the same effect as turning *Campbell*

Soup cans into art, as Andy Warhol did to criticize the culture of popularity.

I could also play the devil's advocate by saying that Rajneesh's moniker as the 'Rich Man's Guru' indicates a man who was as aware as Abraham Maslow was that people struggling to eat will rarely seek spiritual freedom. Happiness and fulfilment are far higher needs in Maslow's hierarchy. Those who have evolved to a higher social stage, however, present quite a conundrum to a mystic hoping to transform humanity. For Rajneesh to address the wealthy without having had creature comforts himself would've been a lack of credibility to convince them of his message.

Perhaps to that end, the Rajneesh brand was evolved into a multi-national corporation. By the time the 1980's rolled around, they had an international footprint. Satellite communes dotted the globe, from the Far East all the way into the America's. Altogether, their spiritual enterprise had several hundred thousand members, all wearing the *mala*, or beaded necklace with a picture of Rajneesh, around their necks. It was their suggestion that Rajneesh adopt the title of 'Bhagwan', which means God.

In its heyday, the collective companies in the Bhagwan enterprise was worth an estimated $60 million, with new publishing contracts for his books reported to have been coming in annually. Their operation extended to restaurants and discos too, all of which served to keep each commune financially self-sustainable.

I remember reading somewhere that the idea to monetize spiritual knowledge was initially given to Rajneesh by one of Laxmi's family friends. She hailed from a wealthy family and, as his first personal secretary, helped to implement a business model that is akin to government taxation. It hinges on a symbiotic relationship where the ashram sees to the needs of the commune by feeding off its people economically, so that growth happened in each mutually.

The wealth associated to the OSHO brand, however, also turned our conversation around the dinner table to the darker side of the commune that was only whispered about.

"[The] exploitation of emotions was His business and He was good at it," writes Ma Anand Sheela in her memoirs about life with Rajneesh.

She still refers to him with a capital H even though Rajneesh publically ridiculed her for abandoning the commune and decamping with millions of their dollars. Still, she was the captain of the commune in its prime, and claimed that the whole thing was a con.

Sheela explains that, particularly amongst educated westerners in the 1970's, group therapies were considered an answer to the maladies of modern man, so people completed them as a way to decorate themselves. "Courses were like medals", she says, which devotees counted as points toward a Bachelor's Degree in enlightenment.

"Some even became addicted to these therapies," she wrote to emphasize the success-stories they liked seeing themselves as. Their participation was overseen by Rajneesh himself on a chart that she regularly prepared for him to show occupancy rates in the various therapy groups.

According to her book, *'Don't Kill Him'*, meditative therapies that were designed to relieve people of anger, jealousy or sexual repressions were a major money-spinner at the ashram. They were offered like "food on a buffet", which is a strategy she attributes to Rajneesh's fine business acumen. He had an acute grasp of the value that meditative therapies had to a commune who were taught by him to despise the word 'ego'.

"In my opinion," she writes, "all these big words [like] ego, meditation and enlightenment, were used to camouflage serious emotions and mask exploitation."

The therapies were expensive too, and Sheela relates how sannyasins coming from the west had lived in the ashram for years without an income. They spent their savings first, and then chose to become beggars in order to remain close to the Bhagwan. Some even turned to prostitution.

Though he inspired such zeal, Ma Anand Sheela said that those who contributed generously to the commune were given 'honorary degrees' in enlightenment. Large donations bought privileges, like access to the Bhagwan, which Sheela says was the beginning of the end. It was initiated by a wealthy set of sannyasins known as 'The Hollywood Crowd', and it was a member of that group who succeeded Sheela as Rajneesh's next secretary. Sheela's robes were publicly burnt to signify the end of her reign.

The commune's controversial Oregon episode is articulated in detail in the Netflix documentary 'Wild, Wild Country', and the skulduggery exposed there is consistent with the insider-accounts of Hugh Milner, another sannyasin-turned-critic. He served as Rajneesh's bodyguard, and described an incident in which he watched an ashram lawyer pour glasses of expensive whiskey to coerce sannyasins into giving up their homes and life-savings for the commune.

In his own book, *'Bhagwan: The God that Failed'*, Milne wrote about how the dental chair in Rajneesh's home came to be there. When the ashram dentist was sent to London to procure it, he was told that the very best reclining chair cost £12,000. Without hesitation, it was paid for in cash, then the astonished salesman was asked to 'muck it up a bit' to avoid the 120% import tax levied on goods brought into India.

Milne observed that sannyasins back then had a messianic zeal for what they found in the Bhagwan. They saw Rajneesh as a jewel that they wanted to gift the world with.

The installation of the dental chair in Rajneesh's home, however, led to Rajneesh allegedly falling prey to a nitrous-oxide addiction that was administered by his own doctors, and is what Sheela was trying to rescue Rajneesh from when she ordered the murder of Rajneesh's personal physician, Amrito, who was ostensibly supplying the drugs.

Milne himself was present on one occasion, when he was asked to photograph Rajneesh in the dental chair. He said that, under the influence, Rajneesh quipped that he was relieved to not "have to pretend to be enlightened anymore."

At the dinner table, we too paused from tearing through the exquisite flatbreads which we used to shovel the delicious South-Indian flavoured meats and vegetables into our mouths. The question between the lines of our conversation asked what we were doing in Pune if Osho himself had indeed lost it?

Traditionally, the sannyasin ceremony was conducted by Osho in group meetings called *dharshans*. Google it for some interesting pictures of the guru transferring energy into the third-eyes of disciples, as part of their initiation. It's a spot between the eyebrows, where the pineal gland is located, and disciples who have experienced it describe it as magical.

Today, the sannyasin ceremony has a statelier look and feel, but the commitments made are just as strong. Moritz and I had watched it together in one of its usual Friday evening instalments.

The glass pyramid in the plaza glowed a mushy pink, while the ashram band hummed dreamily in the background. People were gathered, as if around the campfire, to watch a man sitting cross-legged on a cushion laid down in the centre. In humble white robes, he closed his eyes to imbibe the spirit of meditation. He then made a private vow to immerse himself into the river of life with the trust that it would take him where he needed to go. Gentle a commitment it was, though also one that symbolically cut ties with his collective past that was woven into the basket of his given name. He then took a sannyasin name, and when he stood up, he was born anew as 'Arjuna'.

The name comes after the general of the army that fought the famed *Mahabharata* war in the Bhagavad Gita. Arjuna was hesitant on the eve of the war, since much death was about to ensue by his hand, but he was called to Krishna's feet and schooled in the art of peace. The lesson was that life consisted of both the bitter and the sweet. Duality could not be escaped, so life could only be lived. Participating in it without judgement was the path to becoming a whole man.

That wisdom is one of the reasons why the lotus flower has become symbolic of inner peace. It is a fragrant flower that grows out of a stinking mud, and taking the sannyasin oath reflected the same desire for transformation.

"It's a loyalty programme," Moritz suggested to us around the dinner table.

As an entrepreneur himself, Moritz had a keen eye to spot that the business of knowledge needed to maintain an audience. The sannyasin ceremony fitted well as a customer retention strategy in the broader spiritual business which didn't have Osho as a drawcard anymore.

About that, Naomi Klein cleverly quipped that "we live in a world where we look to corporate brands for poetry and spirituality because we don't get it from our communities, or each other". Her comment makes for an interesting clue as to those who belonged to the Rajneeshee movement.

Picture a typical hippie with loose clothing, long hair and a beard. Those were the symbols of uncertainty, of which there was a lot going around back in the 1960's when the hippies began challenging the stoic values of the Baby-Boomers.

It was a time that evolved out of Elvis Presley's rock and roll era, which was branded as lewd when young girls began feinting from his signature hip-gyrating moves. Rebelliousness was in the air, and the quintessential icon of its spirit was James Dean.

Already in 1952, when Dean starred in *East of Eden*, the sentiment of the youth was gaining traction. *East of Eden* challenged traditional parental wisdom forced upon the youth by Baby-Boomers who, quite reasonably, sought a semblance of order in their lives after a very tumultuous time during the World Wars. In contrast to security, freedom was the value that championed the social revolution of the counter-culture, and deep changes in social values creates uncertainty. Economically, for instance, as what a man consumes changes as he does. I imagine it must have spelt challenging times for the Gillette company which, in 1955, introduced the first adjustable razor to a youth that never shaved.

But it's hard to believe it merely a coincidence that the evolutionary values of the hippies found expression in beards and long hair when that was exactly what Eastern gurus like Rajneesh looked like. He too preached of a more loving and spiritually-aware world in his book *'From Sex to Super-Consciousness'*, which contains messages that match the intentions of the counter-culture who owned the future. I guess all futures are uncertain, and human beings tend to trust familiarity as it provides some predictability.

So, in a way, the criticism that Rajneeshism was a cult, and sannyasins were mindless financial and sex slaves, has another perspective to it. Manipulation could not have only been one-sided, as it seems that Rajneesh and the hippies found each other in the same way that washing powder boxes on a supermarket shelf finds people with dirty laundry. Those boxes have pictures of linens printed on them because products are patterned to the solutions that customers are searching for. It's a mutually beneficial arrangement, so who knows if a guru was made out of a man, or Rajneesh's enlightenment was too mesmerizing to ignore?

Maybe the hippies got more than they bargained for in Osho. By definition, change means an alteration to the identity of an object, circumstance or person –

but an alteration also implies that some of the original characteristics are still retained. Osho however was preaching transformation, which is to evolve into something completely anew.

You can get a glimpse of what that means by doing his *Darkness Meditation*.

On Thursday evenings it was my duty to usher a group of people into a room located in the basement of Krishna House. Once everyone was in, I locked the door and cut the lights. It was so dark in there that it hurt to keep our eyes open. Ordinarily, it's easier to focus on an object since you can direct your attention to it. Darkness however is not an object. It's everywhere, so it can't be seen in the same way that you see an object.

When you close your eyes, you're simply experiencing the negative aspect of light, but that's not 'positive' darkness, the mystic says.

Positive darkness is in fact experienced every day, Osho explained in his book *Meditation: the first and Last*

Freedom. Much activity during the day exhausts your energy, but the darkness of night naturally rejuvenates your body for a new beginning at sunrise. This was the darkness being created in that room as, in nature, all beginnings occur in darkness. Osho described it as delicate and intimate, like a mother's womb.

Sitting with a relaxed gaze, meditators found their eyes getting teary, but keeping both their eyes and themselves open allowed the darkness to enter them. It's a mutual process, since you can't stare into the darkness without it entering you too. The dance of life happens this way. So long as you remain open to it, nature opens itself up to you too. And it was a curious feeling indeed to be enveloped by the darkness. We began dis-identifying with physical forms, including our own bodies, as we felt ourselves dissolving into the darkness.

The meditation was pretty scary for some people, though it's normal for primitive fears which are trapped in our unconscious to arise during its practice. Those fears may even appear as monstrous, and look rather real, but they are really just mental creations. By allowing them to play out, the darkness absorbs them, and eventually you will emerge as a new person, Osho advised.

The silence experienced in the meditation felt uncannily like being in the womb of our pregnant mothers, before our senses were activated by a slap on the bum. That silence is a peek of what life is like beyond the spiritual game we play with ourselves.

It's more pronounced in us, the 'Netflix-generation of spirituality'. In a way, the counter-culture never had to make the choice for a more loving world as it was one defined in opposition to tradition. Millennials today, however, are not looking over their shoulders. Empowered by technology, many possibilities are available to them. But, as Uncle Ben told Peter Parker, with great power comes great responsibility.

Today there are cures to become more passionate if your life lacks lustre, or infuse some stability if it's too exciting. You can improve your productivity, or find ways to deal with stress. Binaural beats for your iPod can help you sleep better, become more energetic, perform sex like a God, or be less anxious about it. A few strikes to a Tibetan bowl can balance your energies, and a lemon can rid your home of bad vibes. You can travel using your astral body, or make your hair grow again on your head rather than from your nose. Ok, I'm joking about that last one, but it certainly is a gap in the market.

A meditation for hair loss, and everything else, in one way or another, is a search for yourself. It is the game of creating ourselves.

For years I was fascinated by prayer. I studied the faces of people in mosques, synagogues, churches, and even those who danced around the fire, if that's how they supplicated. I finally discovered that, behind those closed eyes, was always a request. Begging for forgiveness was asking for dignity, and thanking the Lord was asking for good fortune to continue. Prayer was yet another attempt to create ourselves, and our lives, in the way we wanted.

Sadhguru explained in one of his *Satsang's* that the true desire behind prayer is the power to create wellbeing for ourselves, which translates to pleasant outer circumstances and happy inner climates.

It's sweet, actually, that we have a such a deep yearning to enjoy our lives. We must appreciate the opportunity that life presents, but therein lies the problem of what constitutes pleasant and happy circumstances for you. As individuals, it's our responsibility to decide that, and difficult a task it'll be if you don't know what you're capable of.

That's the real problem. Even religions are solving the problem of identity.

It may come as a surprise that much of the spiritual knowledge that has come and gone is propagating the same solution. It has many variations, and may have even gotten distorted along the way, but the basis has remained the same:

Defining yourself is the quest to discover your highest power, or evolution of yourself.

Theistic religions have resolved that quest with a creation theory, which says that there is a higher power somewhere in the heavens that has created everyone and everything. You can connect with it, call it God, through systems of morality like religion, and so the believer's inner world is one that finds trust in themselves through agency.

Seekers on the hand, as do followers of Eastern religions like Buddhism who don't subscribe to the idea of God, see all of existence as a single organism of which they are a part. They find personal trust by evolving themselves into higher beings that are intrinsically aligned to the power of the whole and, since that affords a capability greater than that of an ordinary man, that state is perceived as divine.

Either way, the results are six and one-half a dozen. No matter what you believe, or what you envisage a greater power to be, the benefit we seek is a higher perspective. It's a better vantage point from which we can see the lay of the land, and with clarity comes the empowerment to fulfil ourselves.

That's essentially the function of an identity.

It's a utility used to navigate life in the world, and we therefore measure a person's character by what they do. The capacity to respond intelligently to life, rather than its usual implication of blame, is what Osho redefined the term 'responsibility' as. It was the basis of his conceptual man, 'Zorba the Buddha', who is a man without limitations, and has an infinite 'response-ability'.

Imagine that through the words of Paramahansa Yogananda who authored the book that was a favourite of Steve Jobs. In *'Autobiography of Yogi'* he describes his initial experiences of enlightenment as escaping the prison of his body, which has outwardly-focussed needs like food. Yogananda found that the world was actually happening within us, and shifting his perspective gave him an awareness of life so complete that he could see a cow behind a wall through the back of his head. His locus of control had extended far beyond the limited vision of his physical eyes and, if you think about it, that's what success really means too.

Think of all that you want to accomplish with your life. Suppose those wishes were fulfilled, what would you want then? Keep playing this game until you can think of nothing more that can satiate you, and you'll find that your ultimate desire is for a limitless existence in which you can create anything.

We all want it all.

We want to connect with others, share with, and love them. We want our lives to be so big that it overflows into the world. In other words, we want to expand to the greatest possibility of ourselves, and that is infinite.

I suppose that is one way to look at the accomplishments of the Osho International Foundation (OIF). In statements made to the

European Intellectual Property Office (EUIPO), its directors showed how they had turned the OSHO brand into a globally-renowned one in relation to meditative products and services. Their publishing catalogue consists of hundreds of books, and even more hours of video and multimedia. It seems that they are fulfilling the vision that was handed to them by their master on his death bed. Osho's last words are reported to have been "I leave you my dream."

Those words, and the circumstances of Osho's death in which they were spoken, are also the source of a heated trademark and copyright dispute that was lodged at the EUIPO by a rival faction of sannyasins. Some of them were once members of the 'Inner Circle', a collegiate of trusted sannyasins appointed by Osho himself. They discovered several years after Osho's death that the commune's legal structures were secretly corporatized outside of India and, today, the revenues earned don't always flow back to the institution. Those who opposed the change were asked to leave, or left on their own accord due to hostilities. Even 'The Hollywood Crowd' stood up one day and left abruptly.

While reading the details of the commune's inner-feud in the book *'Who Killed Osho?'*, it struck me that the kinship I once perceived amongst senior members of the ashram could very well be a façade. The book was written by a seasoned journalist who covered the Rajneeshee story for several years, and the contents of the book articulates various accounts of sannyasins present on the very day of Osho's death. When tallied up, it suggests a conspiracy to hijack intellectual property rights that may have even been in play before Osho died.

It all culminates in the bizarre incident of Osho's Last Will and Testament being produced two decades after his death. Up till then, the OIF had maintained that Osho did not leave a will, but one suddenly surfaced during the dispute at the EUIPO. It stated that Osho, of sound body and mind, had transferred the intellectual property rights of all his works to the OIF willingly, but the will was proven as a forgery and subsequently withdrawn.

Amongst the theories floating in the blogosphere is that Osho was murdered by his own top brass for financial reasons. Another is that Osho was assisted with euthanasia, which was a topic that Osho discussed with his personal physician, and was a conversation secretly recorded by Ma Anand Sheela. Osho could've also accidentally overdosed on drugs, which is a theory connected to fragments of what was possibly spew found on his clothing while being inspected by Dr Gokul Gokani, who signed Osho's death certificate. If actions do speak louder than words then it's also easy to speculate that some senior members of the commune really do agree with Ma Anand Sheela that the whole thing was a con and, angry at being exploited themselves, they decided to claim their share by profiting from Osho's death. Osho could've also died naturally, but few believe the official account of it.

Whichever it was, the Osho institution today seems to be quite a paradox on Osho's actual teachings. He was vehemently against religion itself, let alone establishing one in his name, but in its current configuration the OIF seems to have its own Vatican in Pune, where it has its own currency, clothing, music, rituals and colloquialisms. The only thing missing is a bible, but *'Who Killed Osho?'* mentions instances of instructions being quoted in Osho's name without any real proof as to its origins.

Altogether, it's rather similar to the religion that was allegedly built around Buddha's teachings by the Brahmins when they recognized the opportunity for power in Gautama's death.

The structure and ethos of the Osho enterprise today is comparable to Scientology, which evolved out of a mythology invented by L. Ron Hubbard, and has its own cadre of ex-communicated 'sannyasins' who blew the whistle on its malfeasance. The scientology debacle exposed in Alex Gibney's documentary shares some striking parallels with the OSHO brand's practices, and its wilful demonization of those who don't agree with it.

Like all great brands however, the mythology behind the OSHO brand is an inspiration to many who label themselves as 'Rebellious Spirits'. It's bizarre though that the OSHO brand has made a god out of a man whose message to mankind was that the ordinary human being is divine, and Rajneesh had to have been an ordinary man with ordinary problems himself, or else his words would not have been so incisive for the rest of us.

There are many other questions that *Who Killed Osho?'* asks about the circumstances of Osho's death, which suggests that the institution built around Osho has a character of two faces:

The first is that of a committed and faithful disciple who carried out the master's orders with such zeal that the transformative meditations designed by Osho are accessible to anyone on the planet, and will be for posterity too.

The other face is that of shylock who is feeding voraciously off the master's carcass until it has no more to offer, as the truth is that the source of knowledge that is being offered in the ashram died along with Rajneesh decades ago.

At our table, we laid down our forks and knives. Whether the Osho institution today was a custodian or a duplicitous politician, it was us that either was looking to. We were the ordinary people prospecting for joy in life and even a smidgen of respect for ourselves would be enough to encourage clear distinctions between spirituality and the soothsaying that is often doled out in its name. The objectives of clever entrepreneurship are worlds apart from personal well-being, and it was clear that us seekers had to go beyond a reliance on any enlightened master to find peace and joy in our lives We had to take responsibility for ourselves and so, when the waiter offered desert, we all declined.

But we left Savya Rasa as friends, and waltzed back to the ashram making plans, laughing and joking. The mood was as warm as the Pune night we strolled through. We had found a connection with each other, which was really what we wanted out of our individual spiritual searches, and I suppose it proved that we needn't be sages to enjoy being human. Then again, we are also a mankind who burnt our sisters on the stake, killed our neighbours for being a different colour, and consume an estimated 55 million chickens every single day. Of course, we didn't have to be those people, and that was the sentiment which inspired us to whip our mobile phones and connect on social media.

Lying in bed that night, the words of a Sufi saint who I once interviewed sprang to mind. He smiled at the barrage of questions I was hurling at him, and waited patiently for them to subside. He then said something that defied any story I could tell myself.

He said "in the beginning there was God…nothing has changed."

Chapter Five

The koi fish were startled, and swam to the edge of the pond to see what all the fuss was about. Amrito was a big man, both in stature and authority. He arrived at the Welcome Centre one morning with a stack of pink sheets that were slapped onto the desk before Kushan and Annie. Both of them nodded obediently while he barked instructions, and that was just the beginning of Amrito's tour de force in the WC.

We had it coming too. Earlier, Sheela and I met with him in Lao Tzu House to present our diagnosis of the data errors on her report. Amrito listened for about ten seconds before snapping into 'Doogie Howser' mode. With all the precision of the physician that he was, he broke down the test results into a set of scenarios that were, one-by-one, eliminated until he arrived at the most likely reason for the errors. Unfortunately for the staff in the WC, the logic concluded that it was human error. Amrito was having none of that, especially since the December high-season had already begun, and the ashram saw a steady influx of guests right until the popular Monsoon Festival that happened around February.

Lost in the wake of the storm he raged in the WC was Ameluna. She was the new coordinator appointed after Anurag left, but was also half of Amrito's size, and easily overshadowed by his authority. Ameluna assured him that everything was in order. She had taught before, and had an experience of managing people, but he swung around to me.

I was instructed to copy the training video Carla and I had made to all the registration stations. Amrito didn't want the staff to have any doubts as to the protocol to follow. If you were privy to the meeting Sheela and I had with him though, that really meant "make sure they don't screw up!" I understood the need of course but, without warning, Amrito then put me in charge of the registration staff.

POOF! Amrito disappeared, and suddenly there was calm.

I found Ameluna in the back-office, scribbling furiously in her pocket-book. I had found her like this before, usually when she returned from management meetings. I learnt then that it wasn't the first time she had felt undermined by Amrito.

I didn't tell her that, scarcely an hour before, I met with Sadhana, who served as my WAM coach. I was seeking a transfer out of the WC as, until then, its dysfunctions were the only view of the commune I had. I wanted a fresh perspective. Sadhana though was dismissive, and gave me the impression that the rest of WAM suffered from the same problems, albeit in different forms. Wondering out loud then, I asked how WAM was really structured to teach people meditative skills, and the mumbo-jumbo that came as Sadhana's response sounded suspiciously like WAM being labour subsidized by sannyasin pockets. We decided that I pay the WAM office a visit anyway to see what positions were available. After speaking to Ameluna that day though, I decided to skip the move and accepted Amrito's challenge.

In Ameluna's eyes, I found anarchy. She had something to prove.

Ameluna could be imagined as the new spiritual class emerging in the world today. They are people who've decided that the world did not belong exclusively to capitalists, communists, or anyone. It belonged to everyone, and there was more than one way to live together. Their outlooks are characterized by participation, so I referred to them as 'Neo-Rebels'.

They sound like John Lennon, are disciplined like yogi's, never litter or smoke, and I wouldn't be surprised if they grew their own vegetables. Their wholesome values can be found infiltrating the business world too. The rise of co-ops, in both its profitable and non-profitable variations, are systems of jointly-owned, and democratically run, enterprises. Amongst their founding stories, you'll find that co-ops are often initiated by individuals who have taken the responsibility to create the world they would like to see. The Neo-Rebel, I thought when working with Ameluna, was where Osho's Zen rebellion from the seventies had delivered the world to.

Of course, like all rebels, they also function by disrupting tradition.

For instance, Ameluna was a complete luddite. She despised technology for the interruptions that it caused to human life, but tech is also a cornerstone of life today so she evolved a totally different way of looking at her ambitions. Career decisions were historically based on what activity yielded the most amount of money. A suitable education was then acquired, followed by people gaining experience and walking the road to financial freedom during retirement. Ameluna's ideas about work instead reflected a growing trend today, which sees careers as choosing first what activities most interest people, and then monetizing them through valuable services. The shift was from external dependencies to internal cues, which made the technology used to carry out those services subservient to human needs, and that's how she was an example of mankind's attempt to live more intelligently.

Such conscious approaches to life are empowering and, so today, the development of sustainable solutions rather than rebelling for change the way the hippies did is becoming increasingly popular. With people doing something about it, the notion that the world is a broken and terrible place is challenged.

Take poverty for instance.

When asked why he insisted on meditation while the world was starving, Osho replied that poverty wasn't a disease. In a YouTube video, he explained that poverty was merely a symptom. The root of the problem was greed, which doesn't exist in the world. It's a condition of man, who defends himself against uncertainty by planning for his future. The logical end to that idea though encourages the hoarding of resources, as experienced in capitalism, which in-turn creates the situation of there not being enough to go around. Poverty, in Osho's view, was created by man's greed, which is ultimately a means to cope with survival fears. His solution was to use meditation to evolve people beyond those fears. The symptom of poverty would then disappear.

A similar general shift in consciousness is reflected today in the penetration of yoga and meditation in western lifestyles. Along with all the scientific inquiry into those practices, the Neo-Rebel represents an integration of values from the East and West into a responsible people, and people taking accountability is not a bad direction to go in.

Toward the end of the day, Ameluna shut the door to the WC half an hour earlier than usual. Everyone gasped at her disobedience. How dare she while wearing maroon robes? She set some chairs in a circle over at the pond for us to occupy, and we were then nudged closer until our knees were touching. Ameluna climbed into the circle herself to tell us that working harder in the WC wasn't helping. She recognized a disjointed team when she seen one and, by the time she finished explaining that we simply needed to understand each other better in order to collaborate, everyone breathed a sigh of relief. Gusts of enthusiasm routinely blew through the WC, but invariably waned. We were surprised though when she warned us to only speak when asked to. We were otherwise obligated to listen without question, no matter how the discussion unfolded.

What happened next, thankfully, was just between us and the koi fish.

She began herself by answering two questions: what she liked about working with us that day, followed by what she didn't. When she finished talking, and passed the same two questions over to the person alongside her, you could hear a pin drop. No one dared roll their eyes flippantly. The candour with which Ameluna spoke made the meeting decidedly uncomfortable.

As expected, nothing other than compliments disguised as complaints came out in our first meeting. We just weren't used to the sort of straight-talk that the petite Ameluna with her shaven head was demanding of us, but she persisted, and soon people did open up.

Admittedly, it was difficult to listen to each other sometimes, and altercations did break out as the 'other myself' was exposed. Being forced to wait our turns though helped us to understand the motivations of others, and formulate our responses in a productive manner. It was plain to see that the content of the meeting was not as important as the flow of communication between us, and that nurtured a qualitative change to the way we related to each other.

Now if Sadhana had put it that way during Inner Skills, perhaps 'communicating from the belly' would've made more sense.

This strange meeting came be called the 'Good to be here', and subsequent instalments cut to the nitty-gritty as to why the Welcome Centre was really the armpit of the ashram.

We were six people from the same amount of countries. We didn't share a culture or language, and varied in age by a gap of around twenty years between the youngest and oldest on the staff. Even joking about a guest with a big nose was fraught with misunderstandings because we all had different internal dictionaries that echoed the variety of ways we lived. Overcoming those differences, and acknowledging each other, often led to the 'Good to

Be Here' meetings ending in spontaneous hugs. Really, you'll surprise yourself as to who you become when you feel accepted.

It made a family of us, and earned Ameluna the respect that she wasn't getting in management meetings.

Though the troops were rallied-up, the rote administrative processes that Lao Tzu House asked us to fulfil left us in a catch-22: carrying out the process annoyed guests, but making improvements for their benefit was strongly resisted by the powers that be. What we did instead was capitalize on our own experience as tourists in India.

If you travel to hotels around the world, you'll find that the registration and checkout chores take no more than fifteen minutes each. Since this was the level of service that our guests were used to, we aimed at delivering the same experience. It provided the strategic direction we needed to transform the WC because clarity was not only a moot point for us as staff. The lack of it quickly frustrated guests too.

One question we got all the time was which bench to sit on because reception, payment, and registration were located in different corners of the WC. Even if guests managed to navigate the confusion of presenting themselves at the right place for different stages of the registration process, there were other surprises like not having arrived with the required documentation, or having to run off to an ATM half way through their registrations. Some guests never returned.

Ameluna and I knew that guests simply wanted to gain access to the campus as quickly as possible, but we were beholden to the procedures and layout of the WC. With those constraints being non-negotiable, we shifted our focus from the failures of the Welcome Centre to the fact that we were perfectly poised to assist guests in personalizing their visit to the ashram.

While she ensured the tardy administrative process moved along, I got the team together for regular ten-minute meetings in which the staff were coached on using the registration process to find out what the intentions were for a guest's visit was. It was the kind of customer service training that American brands are famous for, and it empowered the staff to help guests match their interests to campus activities. After all, the value proposition of the business was to deliver spiritual experiences.

We also broke the complicated registration process down into a relay-race with specific engagements about meditations, social life or entertainment that were helpful at different stages of the process. How quickly and effectively we empowered each guest was then measured on a spreadsheet that calculated if we met our 15-minute processing target, and pointed out where we needed to improve.

The magic in the mechanics however was really spun by the staff, who were livelier than ever as they shared their own experiences in order to help guests have a nice stay at the ashram. They effectively instituted a collaboration, and soon the complaints were minimized, transforming the WC from an annoying duty for everyone to a place where people became friends.

While monkeying around in the back-office one afternoon, Ameluna returned to the WC with a paper pad. Our names were written on separate sheets, which were then pasted in a row upon the wall. Having just come back from a management meeting at Lao Tzu House, everyone wondered what trouble we were in now. Ameluna turned to us with a grave look on her face, and asked us to move the sheets bearing our names to a second row every time we left the WC. Everyone sighed, waiting to hear what the point of that administration was. Ameluna then said that the meeting with management had gone rather well, and broke into a smile. On her way back, she had decided to give us some time off to do whatever we wanted. We were to simply use the notes to let others know when we were frolicking about the ashram. When the hoorah's erupted, she quickly warned against a mass exodus.

The staff were delighted to have their work appreciated. It was something that was sorely neglected in the WC before.

It was also a good lesson for Lao Tzu House, that leadership was less about policing a process than it was about unearthing the potential in those who moved it along. It was one of the secrets that Ameluna knew about people, which I discovered when she summarized the management meeting for me using her own experiences of managing people. We concluded that Lao Tzu House's guidance was necessary for the Welcome Centre as they had a lengthy experience in hosting meditators. It struck me then that I had misread her anarchy. She wasn't trying to prove a point at all. She was actually engaging the chaos as a means to observe her own reactions. With her little notebook, Ameluna was using WAM in the way that it was designed.

A little responsibility rubbed off on me too so I remained behind to check emails before leaving, and found that they were still addressed, as always, to 'Dearly Beloved'. But the messages now looked nothing out of the ordinary, and I wondered how I had changed to see them differently. Certainly, the positive feedback we received from guests was a bias upon my mind, but I think the conscious approach we took to improving the Welcome Centre made all the difference.

On any given day, we experience life like the victims of a gestapo firing squad. Hundreds of things are hurled at us. Some are work-related requests that usually come with a sense of urgency. Then there are those little things that are important, like doing the dishes, and while attending to either, we are constantly interrupted by messages disseminated through TV, radio, and the mobile phones we carry all day long. Of course, no man is an island, so you're just one node in a network of people all suffering from information-overload, and all rather happy to delegate some of it to you. We're compelled to respond to at least some of it because we want to, like getting tickets to a concert, but altogether this complexity spells the problems of urgency and importance in our daily lives, and it becomes difficult to give any one thing the attention that it deserves.

The common advice is to prioritize, but that doesn't alter the volume of activity you're compelled to do, so you'll just end up with a backlog of things you feel guilty for not doing. Priority alone doesn't necessarily translate to a balanced lifestyle. Along with it, you also need a process.

Systems like 'Getting Things Done', or GTD, implements such a process for ensuring that the important stuff doesn't slip through the cracks. It even accounts for decisions that may only arise in the future, but could otherwise be kept aside. Other techniques like 'Pomodoro' further instils the discipline to focus on a given task for at least 25 minutes at a time. Software tools like 'Asana' are also popular for integrating the stakeholders in your life with the tasks and available time you have to accomplish whatever you like. Using such tools reassures you that the bigger picture of your life is still safely intact, and that your whole world is not really falling apart as stress often makes us feel. Together, self-management systems aid a conscious approach life. They create balance by addressing not only the content of our activity, but also how we do things.

You don't have to be spiritual at all then to enjoy a good standard of life. Mind you, a good standard of life doesn't equate to a good quality of life.

Walking back to the ashram late one night, I kicked my heels and jumped up to catch a vine hanging from an ancient banyan tree. I swayed above the road like Tarzan, and let go to land a good few paces closer to the ashram. Sniggering to myself as the sting in my feet subsided, I then noticed that I was standing vis-à-vis with one of Pune's dogs.

They're everywhere, and packs of them operated around rubbish bins which were thrown over to spill out the contents. The dogs fed themselves that way, but there probably wasn't much to pick from that night when that malnutritioned one bared its teeth and growled viciously at me.

The street was completely deserted so shouting for help was pointless. My robes also weren't built for speed so making a run for it wouldn't have worked out well. If I took step back, the dog came closer, and if tried side-stepping it, it got ready to pounce. It was by sheer luck that a car pulled out of the hospital driveway and turned in our direction. The moment the headlights were cast on our showdown, we both split in different directions. My heart was still palpitating when I reached the ashram and, bent over to catch my breath, I wondered where the hell all those superhuman meditative skills were when I needed them.

In the old days, our instincts of fight and flight made sense when faced with danger, but that response doesn't apply as well in contemporary times. For instance, if you were insulted by your boss at work, punching him in the face will probably get you fired. You can't suddenly turn on your heels and run away from difficult confrontations either so, today, our flight and flight instincts are often suppressed in social situations - and that affects your health.

Health can be defined as the ability to respond. It is the most the rudimentary definition of life there is, so the quality of our lives doesn't depend solely on organizing our activity. It's really a matter of how conscious we are of what's going on around us.

In truth, information-overload is a small problem. Look around you right now. Everything around, and within you, is available to respond to. The images reflected in your eyes, the scent of the room, the taste in your mouth. Our ability to respond is limitless really. The value of being conscious of the world around us was succinctly clarified by Sadhguru, who used the example of crossing the street. "You don't need to start thinking positively, or start chanting a mantra, to avoid getting hit by the cars," he said, "all that is needed is to look clearly at the way things are."

This is not an exclusively eastern wisdom too. Jack Welch, the former head of General Electric, also agreed that, to get results in life, we should "face reality as it is, not as [we] wish it to be."

The recognition that there can't be any fixed recipe for living gives us the power to see where our attention is needed first before acting. We can then respond to situations as is necessary, which is a more intelligent way to go about life.

Just before lunch, one day, I noticed Carla flying out of Krishna House. The closer she came down the pathway, the more she looked like she was stomping. When she passed by without waving back, I realized that something was wrong, and caught up with her at the main gates to find that a catastrophe had indeed struck.

She'd just found out that her application to extend her stay in WAM had been rejected. Carla had already put a considerable effort into renewing her visa, part of which included a trip to Thailand, which complicated matters even more. Her universe having suddenly shifted left Carla consumed by worry.

When I asked why, she replied that she was accused of being routinely late. That was absurd considering that Carla was especially meticulous about time compared to the rest of us in WAM. She juggled flute-practice with the ashram band alongside her usual duties, and still managed to find time to explore Pune. Calling her out as lazy also seemed petty, then again there are surprise checks in WAM to see if our beds were made. That it was done while we weren't in our rooms was downright disrespectful, so it was easy for me to empathize with Carla, and I offered to help where I could.

"Fuck off!" she yelled.

She blamed my lackadaisical attitude for making her late sometimes and, before storming off, said it was my fault that she got kicked off the programme.

From across the street, Ganeshwari the security guard watched my heart breaking.

Carla's accusations were obviously made in anger, and didn't bother me. She was a grown woman anyway and, even if my punctuality was a problem, I hadn't coerced her into shirking off her duties. What broke my heart was how inept we both were at dealing with life. Dr Wayne Dyer famously said that when you squeeze an orange it's very likely that orange juice will come out. Similarly, and as much as I felt for Carla's predicament, the violence within came out when life surprised us.

We discipline ourselves, sacrifice, and remain patient. We even do the bidding of others in the hope of bringing some stability to our lives in an uncertain world, but an impression of control is only a mask. Deep down we know that we are vulnerable to our lives turning topsy-turvy, at any time, without any notice.

Ghandi's insight was a valuable one when he said that "nothing you do is of any real consequence, but it's very important that you do it."

It implies that all the structures we build around ourselves is only of relative value. Exercise and diet regimes, even brushing your teeth at certain times or in a certain way, are all processes that maintain the structure of our lives in the way we want it. We call them habits, and they develop confidence in our activities. The more of them we have though, the more automatically our attention is diverted to maintaining the structure of our lives, while life itself may be asking for a different response altogether.

Structure in our lives then doesn't translate to fulfilment.

Even productive habits that have sunken into our unconscious, and now happen without our full awareness, are blind spots. The measures we take for stability in our lives eventually become our prisons, by virtue of regulated behaviour that we've chosen for ourselves. And so, by our own hands, we allow our habits to turn us into robots.

Osho gives a poignant example of how destructive this can be in his book *'Awareness'*.

He relates the story of a King who came to listen to the Buddha speak. When Buddha noticed that the King's big toe was waving, it suddenly stopped, and Buddha kept talking. A little later the same thing happened again.

"Why are you doing that?" Buddha asked.

"I wasn't doing it consciously," the King replied.

"This is *your* toe," Buddha said, "and you aren't conscious of it? You may even murder a person without being conscious…"

Edward de Bono describes the conditioning of the mind as throwing a marble into a bowl of jelly. The path that the marble carves alters the shape of the jelly indelibly, and our minds similarly continue to function according to our habits, irrespective as to whether the behaviour is relevant to a situation of not. To combat such stricture, De Bono invented the 'Six Hats' method of problem solving, which is a systematic way of looking at any problem from various internal and external perspectives, to arrive at an informed decision. But this amount of administration is not always necessary if we don't live out of conflicted minds.

You can't ever be the person you intend to be if your mind is constantly steering you in different directions.

That is, by and large, the definition of the problem when we fail to be the people we intend to be, says

Jiddu Krishnamurti, one of the most western-looking of all the eastern sages. He put the problem of conflicting desires into the parlance of our minds, which is a stream of thought that says "I really want this, but that is important too, and what about…"

"We go on falling apart," Osho said about the fragmented mind, body and emotions we ordinarily have. He says it's only natural for an inharmonious life to feel miserable, and like a burden to be carried.

This 'other myself' that's hidden in our automated, and unconscious, behaviours is really just a collection of information gathered by our five senses and recorded in our memories. It knows nothing else so, if we allow it to dictate our lives, it's inevitable that we'll create situations that are simply variations or alternatives to our past choices.

Spiritually-speaking, this is what 'karma' is - the momentum of choices and actions that lead to us feeling trapped in a certain pattern of living. It's quite likely that we will become violent if we suddenly find ourselves in 'habitual' cages. Knowing that we're creating our own problems, but unaware as to how, can leave us feeling rather desperate. In that state it's easy to turn to anyone who is selling what we want to hear.

One evening, I happened upon a chance encounter with the facilitator of the Past-Life Regressions held at the ashram. In the tranquil setting of Dario's Garden Restaurant, he explained that the session aims to help people understand the choices they're making today by delving into their past lives for context. The backstory helps to unearth their motivations so people can navigate out of the trap of cause and consequence, and dissolve their karma.

The girls at the table already knew that much, and had a more pressing concern: were the memories that came up during the session as their past lives in fact true or mere imagination? It was an interesting question as it's rather mysterious to recall a memory as yours but identify yourself as a stranger in it, so how did they really know it was truly their memories?

The facilitator laughed. He probably got that one all the time, and assured the girls that if they remained open to the process, it would all be quite clear to them. That didn't satisfy their curiosity though, and they begged an explanation as to what he meant.

His reply was quite abstract as it's difficult to explain that grand ethereal thing called love. It's the world we want, I suppose, because love is a fitting solution to all the violence we experience. In many ways, we worship it.

To the youth who instigated the counter-culture in the 1960's, love meant the freedom to be themselves. To their parent's generation, the baby-boomers who became intolerant of the World Wars that ravaged their lives, love came to mean security. Today, the neo-rebels are fighting bigotry with the notion that love means sharing and collaboration.

As humanity, we have done much for love through the ages but, while its rich history continues, love has over time also become one of the most contaminated words in our lexicon. It has as many meanings, to as many people, as it reincarnated from one generation to the next. In many ways, love has lost its meaning, so an alternative way to understand this thing we do so much for is through its characteristics.

Put the champions of love side by side and you will find that the baby-boomers, hippies and neo-rebels are all compassionate on one hand, but also decidedly vigilant about a better world on the other. They're continuing a long tradition of love in which vigilance has sometimes won, like during the crusades, and other times compassion, like the work of Mother Theresa. Perhaps it's a coincidence that those two dimensions of compassion and retribution originate in the archetype of God himself in holy scripture, who is the ultimate expression of love our culture knows.

But, in practice, we all also know that love is an act of giving to others what they want rather than holding them up to an expectation of we want, so a love characterized by duality is also a conditional love, and one that the mystics have been discrediting as a fiction. The natural phenomenon of love, the sages say, is an experience of unity between people and everything. Pointing to such experiences is Buddha's sutra, 'Love Yourself'. It's profound because it encourages us to go beyond treating others as we would ourselves, and understand that our sense perceptions can expand to directly experience others as ourselves.

That was the insight to Past Life Regressions that the facilitator was trying to explain. All those disparate events of our current and past lives have a golden thread running through them, and the purpose of the session was to discern how fate was weaving things together to deliver us unto the ultimate destination of all life…unity through love.

The girls suddenly got it, and were delighted that the universe was conspiring to bring about their most heartfelt desires. It lit their eyes, and so the facilitator cordially extended them an invitation to try out the session as soon as possible.

"So, actually, if you can tell how things are connected, then those memories must be real?" one of the girls asked after some careful consideration.

"That's a matter of interpretation," the facilitator curtly replied.

Chapter Six

I got a fright when finding the padlock open. The keys within the security box were missing and the door was left ajar. It was a clear breach of the stringent security protocol that was put in place to protect the memorabilia in Chuang Tzu House. I tiptoed down the stairs into Osho's old home to find the lights still out, but there was some shuffling coming from further within. I crossed the passage quietly and routed through the dental surgery so that I could sneak up to the windows that peeped into the auditorium. There I could decide if ashram security needed to be summoned. When I got there, the apparent burglary ended in a sigh of relief. The new facilitator for the meditation I had regularly assisted with had just arrived early.

"Where are your socks?" she yelled when I introduced myself. The marble in the auditorium was untreated so walking upon it with bare feet was forbidden.

She yanked my sleeve all the way to the basket in the outer hall where we kept a stash of fresh pairs. Along the way, I asked her for the keys to lock the door upstairs, but she wasn't listening. She continued to scold me about the protocol she herself had broken, and then managed to rub me up the wrong way by pulling a smile on her face, gently squeezing my shoulder, and insinuating that my lack of obedience was my ego.

In the ashram, that's code for "it's my way or the highway", and we sometimes joked that they only needed maroon policemen with maroon dogs to formally establish the 'ego police'.

I instantly snapped into the pirate 'Jack Sparrow' while she pulled a 'Miranda Priestly' demeanour, and there it was, the personality clashes that typify all of life. With those masks pulled over our faces, working together became an unnecessary nightmare.

A student once sat before his Zen master and asked if it was proper for a monk to use email. The master replied, "so long as there are no attachments!"

The Gourishankar meditation we were facilitating that night was a process used to create some distance from the thoughts and emotions that make up our experiential realities. It activates what mystics call the 'third eye', or the pineal gland which is located between the eyes. Stepping back allows you to see how the breath itself is not air. Air is only a medium for the life-energy that keeps us alive.

The yogis liken this relationship between life and the body to a rope. If you master the breath, you can follow it out of your body and into a completely different dimension of being. This reflects our spiritual desire to be in our bodies, but experience something greater. Using the breath, we can become amphibious creatures that can venture beyond our physical cocoons, which is why the yogis refer to the breath as 'Koorma Nadi'. The word 'Koorma' means turtle.

The meditation begins by changing the ratio of oxygen to carbon-dioxide in the bloodstream, which makes you feel a little high, like Gourishankar the mountain. This preparation can become taxing too as you repeatedly hold your breath as long as you can, and then continue to keep your lungs empty for as long as possible after exhaling. By then, your body automatically takes care of the next breath as it's gasping for one really.

After about 15 minutes of that, the lights are killed and you spend the next stage of the meditation gazing upon a blue light that strobes at a moderate rhythm. The flashing acts upon the excess of carbon dioxide in the body so, when you stand up thereafter, you feel a subtle tingling. If you surrender to its motions, this energy starts coursing through your limbs, and the experience feels something akin to the shoot of a plant growing out of the ground.

You may have observed how a stalk doesn't shoot straight up. It twirls upon itself to reach higher. It's an analogy I imagined to be what photosynthesis must be like for a plant as it becomes the possibility beyond the limitations of its seed.

The life within us also represents a possibility. We humans have evolved minds over time that afford us much higher possibilities than, say, cockroaches who are programmed for survival. They do it very well, but don't have the discretion that our minds allow. With the power of choice, we can create ourselves in any we want, and attain higher possibilities like love or freedom. But choice is also the reason for all seeking, spiritually or otherwise.

In one his *Satsang's*, Sadhguru explains that some people seek merely an escape from their in-laws and other humdrums of life. Others are looking for change. They want to improve the situations in their lives, usually to more peaceful or loving ones. Those wishing to transform though don't want anything of their old selves remaining. They are in search of a whole new life, like amphibians that evolved from fish. All forms of seeking though are for a more enhanced experience of life. Even drink and drugs are consumed for that reason, but seeking only becomes relevant once you become aware of your limitations, the greatest of which is your own death.

Ameluna was especially animated as we walked to the Burning Ghats on Pune's riverbank one night. She had attended Osho's funeral back in the nineties and described the procession as one that flooded the streets and stopped the constant traffic on North Main Road. Thousands of people in white robes were laughing, singing, and dancing. They didn't stop rejoicing either when the body of their master was laid down on a stone platform, garnished with flowers, and sent off into the unknown by a pile of burning logs. Osho's cremation was celebrated by sannyasins as much as his life was.

To them, death was no more than a fiction.

It is one of the central ideas that characterizes the commune Rajneesh built. In his talk *'The first principle'*, he said that birth was not the beginning of life and neither was death its end. Life existed beyond them. Birth and death existed as events within life, but life itself was not born and does not die. Life, he said, simply endures. It was a misunderstanding to think of death as a destination like heaven or hell. He described it as a boundary to be crossed, one that takes us beyond the limitations of our physical bodies, and into the realm of infinite possibilities.

Ordinarily, our physical needs for food and shelter create the situation in which the possibilities of our lives are determined by lack, and that in-turn defines the type of seeking that we undertake.

Poverty will result in a search for wealth, and loneliness for a relationship. The objects of desire however only change the direction of our efforts, but the process of seeking to satisfy a lack remains the same. The pattern of life we then live is feeling limited in some way, desiring an outcome beyond it, and then trying to attain it using whatever means we have at our disposal. It's an endless process because life has much to offer, and the objects of our desires are infinite.

A fulfilled desire too is as frustrating as an unfulfilled one. The moment we achieve something, we immediately earn the perspective to see something even more valuable, and so, new desires are born. It's not an altogether bad thing. Desire is life. It takes us progressively from point A to point B, but getting stuck in the pattern of constantly seeking more can be very unsatisfying. Eventually, we tire from the incessant search and peace becomes the object of our desire, but it can't be attained by using the same slavish process that we seek relief from. To be peaceful, the ones in the know say that we have to change the process.

Death was a founding principle of Rajneesh's commune because it initiates that alternate process of living beyond the cycle of desire and attainment. The meditations practiced at the ashram are ways of voluntarily withdrawing support for our wants - in fact, making every effort to destroy them as liberty is the opposite of self-preservation.

In effect, Rajneesh was really teaching his people to die.

Not literally of course. His meditations were a method to peek beyond the wall of our personalities. Once we do, he explained, we would instantly realize that our bodies and personalities are only transient, and we ourselves endured nevertheless.

In that way, death was merely a fiction.

I waved at China-Babu as Ameluna and I strolled past his ramshackle restaurant on Lane A. We became friends late one night, when his momo's and egg-fried rice was the only food in sight. Though hungry, I was paranoid about getting the 'shits', and insisted on inspecting his wok to see if it at least looked clean enough for a western palate. Of course, I was under the delusion that I would instantly recognize the dysentery there without a microscope, but he understood immediately and proceeded to wash the wok with the same tap-water I was warned would give me the shits.

Death too needn't be taken so seriously, Osho repeatedly said. Being a playful guy, he penned a quirky epitaph for himself that reads: 'Osho, never born, never died, only visited this planet.'

Sannyasins also don't ever refer to Rajneesh as having died. Instead they say that he 'left his body', and that's an interesting colloquialism to understand what enlightenment actually is. Academically it's described as transcending the usual operations of the body-mind and living from what the mystics call 'no-mind', but that's a difficult thing to conceive without an actual experience of it. More helpful perhaps is an inquiry into what the awakened ones are actually enlightened about.

Krishnamurti defined it as the realization of there being no self to be enlightened in the first place. Strange as that sounds, he explains that there is no distinction between you and your higher perspective. Only our minds see things in terms of duality.

For instance, if you were a non-violent person, and wanted to become violent, then you've created a trajectory of time in which you will be transitioning from non-violence to violence. Effort then becomes your focus. You may sign up for CrossFit, or learn how to cuss, but either way Krishnamurti calls this effort being in a state of 'becoming'. The fact of the matter is that you as a violent person is only a projection of the mind. It represents where you want to go, but you as a non-violent person is the fact. Acknowledging the fact rather than the projection is to recognize life outside of the psychological structure we call time. To Krishnamurti, perception is action, and so to be awakened then is simply having the clarity to see life as it actually is.

Back at the ashram, Ameluna and I wandered through the gardens while tallying up all that had transpired in the Welcome Centre, and what plans the experience had hatched for our respective futures. I only had a couple days left so it seemed like the opportune time for her to relay a message that asked me to continue helping out in the WC thereafter.

I didn't know where the request originated from, but the fact that it came put a smile on my face. It was a testimonial that confirmed the Welcome Centre was better than we initially found it, and that was what I had set out to do in the first place. Naturally, I was curious as to what type of help was wanted of me.

Before we got into that though, Ameluna sheepishly added that the ashram welcomed my help on condition that I paid for any additional days I remained on campus. It wasn't their policy to grant concessions to anyone, even those they were asking a favour of.

I laughed, thinking that she was pulling my leg, but it was a moment in which I was once again betwixt by what was true and what was not.

The request could be read in several ways. It could be the arrogance of a business which was still pretending to be commune and attempting to manipulate my interest in Osho to score a freebie. It could also be an invitation to contribute to a cause that they had been mandated with, and felt was worthy. There could also be a hundred other motivations for the offer but, being neither a critic nor sympathizer of Osho, I really didn't know what to make of it.

I sat down.

Actually, the conditions of their offer smacked of the same situation I was in when finding my friends slandering me behind my back. Those friends too were only prepared to accept me under conditions that suited them. This request, however, came from complete strangers, so I wasn't invested in them, and that helped me to see things differently. I realized that I was free to let anyone disrespect me. At least then it would be clear as to where we all stood and why.

Admittedly, it was a bitter truth to accept that society works by only accepting those whom they share similar values with. I suppose finding relationships that support our deeply felt notions does lend a sense of permanence in an otherwise uncertain life but, look around, each of us grows in our own way. There was nothing to say, forgive or do. The only thing left was a good enough reason to keep walking.

I didn't know it then, but this was the insight into integrity that I was looking for all along.

The next morning, I attended the last instalment of Inner Skills, in which the class was split into two groups. Amrito whispered to us that those in the other group were being instructed to become human statues which we could mould in any way we liked. They were being told to be receptive and allow the fun the exercise was meant to be. None of them, however, were expecting us to twist them into the most embarrassing positions ever. In fact, Amrito told us, the obscener the better. Indeed, it was a fun exercise, until we got our turn to be statues.

I'm willing to bet the other group was told that this was their chance to show us what being cruel really meant. And they really did improve on our ideas of obscenity. Members of the alternate group laughed and jeered as they walked around to inspect the statues. Some whispered to their friends and sniggered as they waltzed by, while I watched them torment me because I had to - my eyes we sculpted to remain open. Even though I knew their taunting was part of the exercise, it still hit a nerve…yes, that one, the one that nags you to improve.

When life doesn't go the way we want it's easy to think, at least to some degree, that God or nature didn't do a good enough job on us. Why would we ever want to change ourselves if we didn't think that we were deficient in some way? To become better is then a form of dignity we intend to gift ourselves with.

Given the circumstances, I had none of it. And, really, I knew this moment was coming from somewhere deep down in my gut. I was bent over with my cheek to the floor, one hand twisted awkwardly behind my back as a lever for submission. My tormentor might as well have pulled out a compass to spread my knees in the way that he carefully did and, when finally satisfied, he left me in a sadomasochistic stance fit for a pornographic website.

Gee, even love doesn't have us do the things we do for God!

Mirek, my sculptor, whispered to me that it was a position in which he'd never felt more vulnerable. It was interesting that his cruelty was expressed sexually, my mind was saying in a British accent, but he made that confession like we were discussing the weather. It rang true. There was no pretension in his humiliation and, in a moment of lucidity, it was impressed upon me what integrity really was.

Everything we achieved in the Welcome Centre was not possible without it. Integrity was simply when thought and emotion were aligned to intention so that the action which followed was true. It's being coherent, and no one who is sincere ever feels like a fake because integrity is not about how you are when others are watching. It's about how you are within yourself.

That's saying a lot when you're bent over like a porn star.

The next day was my last, and I checked emails for fun. The first I read was an angry one, written in response to the spreadsheet I sent out as my parting gift. I hoped that management would build upon the improvements we made in the WC as it really inspired the staff, but everyone didn't receive my sentiment the same way. The words in that email yelled that it wasn't my place to question anyone. The person who wrote it had obviously assumed that I implied they weren't doing their jobs properly but, when I got to the end of the rant, I realized that it was the first email I had come across that didn't begin with the customary salutation 'Dearly Beloved'.

I appreciated the sincerity of it, and remembered why the phrase stood out for me in the first place.

To use the word 'beloved' is a rather personal way of addressing an audience as compared to, say, the genteel equivalent of 'Ladies and Gentlemen'. The operative words in the latter phrase are concepts that refer to the type of people that can be found, but lacks all the chemistry of actually being with other human beings. "My beloved ones," was the way that Rajneesh began his discourses in his early days, and remains the opening lines of the book that catapulted him onto the world stage. That book was *From Sex to Super-consciousness'*, and it spoke about how the biological chemistry responsible for sexual attraction is only a gateway to the many ways that consciousness expresses itself…

The rant in the email I was reading exposed a lunatic. Ameluna was a force of determination. Sheela was gentle, Amrito a fire, Kushan was a great joker, Anurag an archetypal mother, Amara an engineer, Annie a cautious soul, Saroja teemed with adventure, Tathagat a connoisseur, Carla a warrior, and everyone else too were inexplicably themselves.

Carla eventually was victorious in having her stay at the ashram extended, after the 'mistake' was rectified. Last I saw her, she was in silence. She had joined a course that was designed to undo the hypnosis of the past, and I wondered who she may emerge as when all was said and done.

Even in such a small commune, everyone was their own person, so just imagine a world pregnant with diversity.

At the ashram's restaurant, a whole group of us fell together one afternoon. Many of us were leaving, and so shared our opinions about the ashram. Ivan had acquired a sense of humour, and didn't have to say a word to serve as a positive review for Osho's meditations. Others were concerned about costs, and decided to pursue personal growth in Delhi or Goa, where other centres in the Osho eco-system provided the same meditations at a discount. Still, there were some who enjoyed the experience, but reduced the Pune ashram to a ski resort, albeit with a spiritual theme. Some were coming back to dance, others to see friends, while those serious about the subtle art of dissolving their personalities discussed enlightened masters who are alive today, and were still actively guiding seekers.

From our conversation, I gleaned that Rajneesh and the spiritual rebellion that he instigated was relevant for his time, but the world had moved on since. Rebelliousness had served its purpose, but the 'Netflix-generation of spirituality' were not unlike the first sannyasins who built the commune with Osho. They too seek a sense of connection that has been completely sanitized from the commune in its incarnation as a meditation resort. It's ironic that the effort to make Osho's work globally accessible actually lost the spirit that so many visit his ashram for.

In the end, I think Kala was right. The experiences we have are really what we make of them, and for that reason it's perfectly ok to dance around the fire, jump up to scream 'Hoo', or engage in any other tomfoolery for that matter. All of it is useful to discern the path that is right for you. Even if you are a victim of a clever entrepreneur, it's nothing that a little attitude adjustment can't fix. There is no harm in opening yourself up to the journey because there is no purpose in life according to Zen. All we can do is simply play with it.

That is rekindling the sense of wonder we once had when we were children ourselves.

Osho explained that all religiousness is the reclaiming of our childhoods. We have to return to the points where our energy was diverted from its natural course, and relive all those painful memories that were repressed. In facing them bravely, we create the eyes to undo the things that suffocate us into miniscule possibilities.

As far as Osho goes, it's hard to say who he really was because we often see what we want to in others. The mystics also tower above us in experience so we only understand them through our own perceptions of the world. Sometimes, they seem so different that we may even be offended by them, and that's perfectly fine if we don't allow the prejudice to interfere with what can be learnt.

Imagine it from their perspective. Mystics are those trying to communicate to people who only understand words something that cannot be communicated in words. It sounds frustrating, funny even, but I think it cuts right down to the real issue…that it must take an incredible amount of courage to simply be yourself because it'll make a stranger of you, and we are so afraid of being alone that we would rather live in madness than accept ourselves the way we are.

And Osho was perfect example of a sore thumb. The facts that tell the biography of an Osho, or a Jesus for that matter, sum up men who dared to be themselves, and though that made them the greatest strangers in the world, would you rather endure your days meekly or squeeze every last drop out of life?

It's your choice, and is why anyone can understand Osho when he said that the only thing equal about us all is our individual uniqueness. "You are you, and I am me," he said.

I left tea and poppadums at the poolside to go pack my bags. The entire meaning of my life at that point hinged on finding a reliable cab to make my flight in the wee hours of the morning because, in India, 4 a.m. could mean 4-15, 5 a.m., or not arriving at all.

As I strolled into the dusk, the insects buzzed as they usually do on warm evenings in Pune. I weaved dreamily along the white stone pathway toward Buddha Grove. In it, I saw the silhouette of a figure just beyond the trees. In the twilight, it appeared almost gossamer, and kept my attention. Closer down the pathway, the silhouette gained definition, and I found myself looking at the delicate frame of an elderly man wrapped in a lunghi and chadrah. Those are the traditional loincloths that Indians wrap around their waists and the shawl they throw over their shoulders. A sudden gust of wind blew the man's long white beard over his shoulder and, as he reached over to catch it, I caught a glimpse of his huge glaring eyes. When they met mine, I recognized him from the hundreds of pictures of the deceased master that I had seen, and I waved him goodbye.

I knew he was just a mirage.

But an Osho is also a map for rebellious spirits, a Krishnamurti one for the intelligent. A Sadhguru is a map for those seeking practical possibilities, and an Eckhart Tolle is one that can guide you to gentleness.

The Lao Tzu's, Gautama's, Abraham's, Jesus's and Mohammed's are all unique creations of life, who is the greatest teacher of all. In its wisdom, it made us unique too.

Thousands of years ago, when Buddha asked people to be a light unto themselves, he meant that we shouldn't rely on anyone for our wellbeing. That includes the mystics. Indeed, we need them as Sherpa's in the unseen world, but our lives are no else's business but our own. Errors and omissions accepted, to navigate life using our own devices is an empowering stance, for mistakes are a way to grow. In fact, if you've read this far, don't take my impressions to heart either. Find your own truth. It is a gift that only you can accept, and once you acknowledge yourself, nothing's the problem.

Who knows what possibility you truly represent?

The only one that matters is the one that you are. Truth itself, the masters say, cannot be transferred. That's why dogs sniff each other's backsides and, similarly, entire books can be written about the taste of an apple, but it still won't substitute for just one bite.

At 4 a.m. the next morning, I watched a clean-shaven man slap some cologne onto his cheeks to wake up. The woman mopping the floor around him was doing it with her eyes closed, until the mop hit a pram, and the face of the baby inside began wailing, waking us all up. The mother radiated a gentle smile as she cradled the child in her arms, not noticing a group in suits and ties assembling in the queue before her. Their faces looked anxious, and were ushered into the queue by airport officials who looked as stoic as airport officials do. The man selling roti's to them had anticipation written on his face, and relief became the face of the man who bought one. Around me in the airport, some faces were long like a giraffe's, others round like a chipmunk's, still some looked like rats and bears and dogs and cats.

Looking into the eyes of all of them, I couldn't help but wonder what it was that I was actually looking at. They were people, no doubt, but I had come to understand that the body was only a vessel for the life within. The same life could be found in the private worlds behind the eyes of insects, in the rustling of the trees, or the steadfastness of a rock. It could sometimes be felt, if I was receptive to it, and so I continued taking a long hard look at all those faces for, somehow, I was seeing myself in them too.

In the end, everyone needs everyone. Even if we do succeed in creating a better world, it will still be one in which everyone needs everyone. It's just a fact of life that there is no choice but interdependence, and there is every choice to lead.

Life is not a noun. It's a verb, Osho said, which has consequences, so it's imperative that we be honest with ourselves as to who or what we are, and open enough to neither judge ourselves nor put our heads in the clouds. This was the sense of candour that was really needed.

And sincerity is the key.

It's a compass to navigate through the forest of only seeing what we want to see, and telling ourselves the stories that we want to hear. If anything, the one person who is worth not deceiving is ourselves because the entire quest, I've found, is a 'who' question. It's about identity, and you don't have to learn or do anything to discover yours as a simple heart already knows the rhythm of life. That's probably why the mystics refer to self-actualization as less of a discovery than it is a remembering.

To them, enlightenment can't be attained like practical goals. It's something that happens naturally while you're walking along your way. That nature intended us to arrive at some wonderful destination is, I guess, again a reason to ask if that is what we want to hear while growing the courage to deal with contemporary life.

Of course, whether Rajneesh, or any of these people are enlightened, I don't know. I don't even know if enlightenment exists as a phenomenon, but I did find consistency in the teachings of the mystics. Their messages can be summarized as just three basic ideas: Firstly, we don't see life clearly because we've invested ourselves in thoughts and things that we've taken as ourselves. Next, we've fashioned those identifications into a personality that deludes us into thinking that there is any life outside of this very moment. And lastly, in this moment you will find that the source of the whole of existence is within you.

Looking at ourselves as such immense possibilities provides a very different perspective on the ambitions that we're constantly told to want.

It's true that success is a wonderful feeling, but whatever can be conceived as being successful is still a boundary that we draw around ourselves. Life can't be fulfilling if we're constantly settling for small joys, and what are they really besides the things that we see other people do and have? Bursting with life is venturing to places which we haven't even imagined yet. Hopefully, there you'll stumble upon the life beating within you.

Isn't that the most important thing?

If I went back in time, and told caveman that I have a device in my pocket that could make fire, he would probably laugh. The moment I struck a match though…

In unawareness, we miss the most provocative mysteries of life. I guess we bring it upon ourselves because the world we live in is not kind to those who admit that they don't know. But ignorance is full of possibilities. In it can be found delightful mysteries, like how a blade of grass is as important to our existence as we are to it. Or what about the space that lies between those two? It is something that we know is there but don't fully understand. Without curiosity we miss that we are so intrinsic a part of life that we are anchored in it, as if our lives are the words of nature's conversation. And without any foregone conclusions it's easier to see that, no matter what religion or denomination or cult we come from, as people we have this yearning within to somehow rise above all the malady of life. If we have that yearning then somewhere within us, however feint, there must be a knowing of something beyond. That knowing, I guess, is why Osho said that we already are the people we dream to be. That we are enlightened, and that we just have to come to realize it.

See, Dearly Beloved's, that's just like finding out the truth about the Easter bunny.

THE END.

I hope you enjoyed this story!

Please write a review on my website, GoodReads, or the marketplace where you purchased this book from. Your feedback helps me to write the stories that you like.

Find my books on Amazon, Smashwords, Kobo, the Apple store and many libraries. Or stay updated on my new books, artworks and other creative products by connecting with me:

Newsletter: subscribe at whiteteastudios.com

Twitter: @yousuftilly

Facebook: facebook.com/whiteteastudios

Website: www.whiteteastudios.com

More by Yousuf Tilly

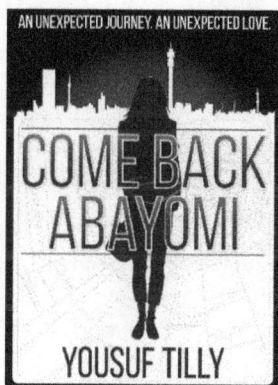

BAD LOVE

Who do you sleep with?

When the universe shifts, a young writer struggling to express himself suddenly drops into the magical world of an exorcist. He finds himself pinning down a frail woman with five men and, while wondering what the hell he's doing, comes face to face with the devil possessing her. As the clues to exorcise her unfold, dark family secrets come to light, and the writer questions whether people are worse than the devil?

Readers Say:

"First I thought it was a joke, then..." "Didn't see that coming!" "I was spellbound, pun intended!" "Loved this story…I want more!" "Came back to re-read this story numerous times."

Read it online now:

https://whiteteastudios.com/books/

COME BACK ABAYOMI

An unexpected journey. An unexpected love.

High-powered attorney at law, Abayomi, is still an authentic African woman. She's invited to South Africa on a diplomatic mission, then gets abducted in a xenophobic attack. In a travel adventure through historic Johannesburg, Abayomi finds herself tangled in an unfolding conspiracy of political big-wigs, priests and immigrant children. Then again, she's dangerously drawn to her kidnapper when she senses a man beneath the beast. To trust her instincts or not, that is the journey of a capable woman challenging male dominance.

Readers Say:

"The unspoken passion is a winner." "Abayomi is big enough to say this is who I am." "He's aloof and mysterious, the type of guy who wants to do good but doesn't know how." - More reviews online.

Read a sample chapter now:

https://whiteteastudios.com/books/

List of References

Chapter Two

- "Meditation: the first and last freedom" by Osho

- https://www.osho.com/read/osho/osho-on-topics/ego

- https://www.osho.com/iosho/library/read-book/online-library-ego-intelligence-become-0b5ced57-f5f?p=7a9b3ce8e4dbc1082e28ee63096db498

- "The fish in the sea is not thirsty" Talk 12, by Osho.

- Conversations with the Mystic, Sadhguru and Vinita Bali:

https://www.youtube.com/watch?v=PHvHMiPi
Kao

Chapter Three

- "Talks on death" by Osho (36 Chapters)

Chapter Five

- "Awareness" by Osho.
- https://lifelessons.co/spirituality/sadhguru-2-2/
- https://youtu.be/smPVh4vg66M
- https://youtu.be/FBYoZ-FgC84
- https://youtu.be/0btJHqGY0l8

Chapter Six

"The First Principle, Talk 9" by Osho.

Meditation Around the World

Osho and Osho Centres

- https://www.osho.com/meditate/places-to-meditate/meditation-centers
- https://www.osho.com/meditate
- https://www.osho.com/visit

Sadhguru and the ISHA Foundation

- https://isha.sadhguru.org/in/en/center

- https://isha.sadhguru.org/in/en/sadhguru/mission/isha-foundation
- https://isha.sadhguru.org/in/en/sadhguru

Paramhansa Yogananda and the Self-Realization Fellowship

- http://www.paramhansayogananda.com/
- http://www.yogananda-srf.org/SRF_Centers_and_Programs.aspx

Krishnamurti Foundation

- https://www.jkrishnamurti.org/worldwide
- https://www.jkrishnamurti.org/teachings

Eckhart Tolle and the ET Foundation

- https://www.eckharttolle.com/

- https://www.eckharttolle.com/search-local-group/
- https://www.eckharttollefoundation.org/

Ramanamaharshi

- https://www.sriramanamaharshi.org/
- https://www.sriramanamaharshi.org/ashram/visiting-us/

Alan Watts

- http://www.alanwatts.org/

Mahavatar Babaji and Bhakti Marga

- https://sadhana.bhaktimarga.org/compare-sadhana-practices
- https://www.bhaktimarga.org/bhakti-marga/global

Sri Yukteshwar and Kriyananda

- https://www.sriyukteswar.com/
- https://www.ananda.org/about-ananda-sangha/

Lahiri Mahasaya

- https://www.lahiri-mahasaya.org/

Ramakrishna

- https://www.ramakrishna.org/
- https://www.ramakrishna.org/act_srv.htm

Good luck with your inner exploration!